TALKING ABOUT
FILMS

CHIDANANDA DAS GUPTA

TALKING ABOUT FILMS

ORIENT LONGMAN

Talking About Films
Chidananda Das Gupta

© 1981 ORIENT LONGMAN LIMITED

Regd. Office
3/5 Asaf Ali Road, New Delhi 110 002

Other Offices
Kamani Marg, Ballard Estate, Bombay 400 038
17 Chittaranjan Avenue, Calcutta 700 072
160 Anna Salai, Madras 600 002
1/24 Asaf Ali Road, New Delhi 110 002
80/1 Mahatma Gandhi Road, Bangalore 560 001
3/5/820 Hyderguda, Hyderabad 500 001
S. P. Verma Road, Patna 800 001

Printed by S. K. Ghosh at the Calcutta Press Pvt. Ltd.
and Published by Sujit Mukherjee
Orient Longman Ltd.

To Rina

⚘ acknowledgements

M any friends helped me with this book and I would like to convey my appreciation to them. I would like to thank in particular Rita Ray (better known as Kobita Sarkar) for lending me a number of stills and photographs and also Purnendu Pattrea, the well-known artist and film-maker, who very kindly undertook to design the cover and to prepare the artwork for the photographs used in the book.

preface

I ndia's Independence somehow launched me into an irrepressible enthusiasm for the cinema. It was in October 1947 that some of us, including Satyajit Ray, got together and started the Calcutta Film Society in an attic in Ballygunge where I used to live. It was a period of discovery. Suddenly we saw what the cinema could mean and how different it could be from what went under its name.

In a country fed mostly on imported escapist films and their inept local imitations, the exposure to *Battleship Potemkin* and *Nanook of the North, Night Mail* and *Un Carnet de bal* brought about a burning desire to tell everybody what a great art the cinema was, and to prove, in the shortest possible time, that great films could be made in India — films that would shake the world and change our own country. With our group were associated some of the best known names of Indian cinema today. Besides Ray, there were Ritwik Ghatak and Mrinal Sen, Subrata Mitra, Bansi Chandragupta and Hari Sadhan Das Gupta — people who were later to climb varying heights in film direction, cinematography, art direction, and documentary film-making. The list is by no means complete. And where would the makers of the new Bengali cinema have found their nourishment without their Calcutta Film Society, especially in the years between Independence and the First International Film Festival in 1952? By 1956, with the success of *Pather Panchali*, first at home and then abroad, the film society scene opened out and took on an almost formidable aspect. Enthusiasm for the cinema became respectable, and a wide range of people rushed into film societies.

Besides being the general factotum of this burgeoning group, the 'fall guy' who was always pushed into doing the secretary's chores for the Calcutta Film Society and later for the Federation of Film Societies of India, I was also its chief scribe. I wrote ceaselessly, with missionary zeal, in praise of good cinema, for upwards of twenty years. It was a sort of battle — sometimes shadow-boxing — against what one thought was ignorance, lack of vision.

Writing on the significance of Ananda Coomaraswamy's ideas in our time, K. G. Subramaniam shrewdly points out that Coomaraswamy's vision of once great civilizations going astray turned him into a polemicist of sorts, and 'all polemicists tend to be contained by the questions they are trying to counter'. Coomaraswamy overcame this problem with the great authority of his scholarship and his analytical ability; lesser mortals have often found their polemical bent robbing them of a breadth and freedom of thought essential to good criticism.

This was the fear that beset me in making a collection of my essays on the cinema and prevented me from publishing them as a book for a long time. Finally I mustered enough courage to select the ones that seemed to be the least tainted by the zeal of a mission and to retain some relevance. 'Publish and be damned' said a friend one day, and suddenly the words fell on a receptive ear.

Taken from writings published over a long period in newspapers and periodicals in India and abroad, these essays range over a variety of subjects, but are by no means comprehensive or integrated into a structure. For instance, there is a longish piece on Satyajit Ray but relatively brief discussions of Ritwik Ghatak and Mrinal Sen. Besides, I have made no attempts to update the articles. Thus the essay on Ray deals only with the first ten years of his work. There is no discussion of Mrinal Sen after *Bhuban Shome*. The seventies have been eventful enough in any case to warrant a separate volume.

So, except for a reference to one film festival in the seventies, this book concerns itself either with thoughts on world cinema which illuminate the Indian condition or events and films in the Indian scene of the fifties and sixties. To these two strands, I have added another, a more personal one; what was so far the diary of a film critic turns into a rumination of a new entrant into film-making. It was a period of some significance, which saw the crystallization of ideas on the future of the new Indian cinema, and the rise of some of the stalwarts who continue to dominate and provide the points of reference for later movements, including those that veer away from it.

Many of the essays in this collection are enlarged and rewritten versions of articles that appeared in various newspapers and journals earlier. Some of them are the result of the combination of different articles. However, as far as my records are correct, the original essays appeared as articles in *Film Quarterly* (University of California Press), *Indian Film Review, Indian Journal of Music, Span, Seminar, The Illustrated Weekly, The Statesman, Amrita Bazar Patrika, and The Hindustan Times.*

If there is a common thread running through these essays, it is probably that of the two main concerns — one for the creative cinema which has resulted from some social engineering since Independence, and the other for the mass cinema which has been left to its own devices — trying to come together into one unified understanding. It is as yet an uneasy union, but one that seems worth seeking.

New Delhi, 1980 CHIDANANDA DAS GUPTA

was so far the diary of a film critic turns into a rumination of a new entrant into film-making. It was a period of some significance, which saw the crystallization of ideas on the future of the new Indian cinema, and the rise of some of the stalwarts who continue to dominate and provide the points of reference for later movements, including those that veer away from it.

Many of the essays in this collection are enlarged and rewritten versions of articles that appeared in various newspapers and journals earlier. Some of them are the result of the combination of different articles. However, as far as my records are correct, the original essays appeared as articles in *Film Quarterly* (University of California Press), *Indian Film Review*, *Indian Journal of Music*, *Span*, *Seminar*, *The Illustrated Weekly*, *The Statesman*, *Sunday*, *Filmfare*, *Patriot*, and *The Hindustan Times*.

If there is a common thread running through these essays, it is probably that of the two main concerns — one for the creative cinema which has resulted from some social engineering since Independence, and the other for the mass cinema which has been left to its own devices — trying to come together into one unified understanding. It is as yet an uneasy union, but one that seems worth seeking.

New Delhi, 1980   CHIDANANDA DAS GUPTA

ಬಾ contents

Preface   vii

Indian Cinema: High and Low

The Cultural Basis of Indian Cinema   3
In Defence of the Box Office   18
Music: Opium of the Masses?   29
The Futility of Film Censorship   40
Barua: Legend and Reality   49
Satyajit Ray: The First Ten Years   55
Bengali Cinema: In and out of the Ray Umbrella   76
Are Film Societies Necessary?   93
The Golden Age of Indian Cinema: Still to Come?   **103**

Speaking in General

What is a Good Film?   111
The Story and the Film   122
The Screenplay as Literature   128
The Documentary : Art or Propaganda   134
Films Remembered   142
Cinema in the Sixties: Some Trends   156
Notes on Russian Cinema   169

In a Personal Vein

From Advertising to Films   179
Dance of Shiva: Postscript to a Film   187

A Select Bibliography   197
Index   199

contents

Preface vii

Indian Cinema: High and Low

The Cultural Basis of Indian Cinema 3
In Defence of the Box Office 13
Music: Opium of the Masses? 20
The Futility of Film Censorship 30
Drama, Legend and Reality 49
Satyajit Ray: The First Ten Years 55
Bengali Cinema: In and out of the Ray Umbrella 76
Are Film Societies Necessary? 93
The Golden Age of Indian Cinema: Stilled, Come? 105

Speaking of Cinema

What is a Good Film? 116
The Story and the Film 142
The Screenplay as Literature 248
The Documentary: Art or Propaganda 134
Films Remembered 212
Cinema in the Sixties: Some Trends 126
Notes on Russian Cinema 169

A Personal View

From Advertising to Films 179
Those in-Shift: Fragment to a Film? 187

A Select Bibliography 197
Index 199

Indian Cinema : High and Low

～ the cultural basis of
Indian cinema

'We must put everything into the cinema,' says Jean-Luc Godard, the high priest of modern cinema. And his films leapfrog from real life to painting, literature, advertising, science, politics—connecting it all less and less by story links, and more and more by the unifying force of the film-maker's mind, turning narrative, 'objective' cinema into a direct personal communication between the film-maker and his audience. But this 'putting everything into the cinema' is only made possible by the film-maker's awareness of the many past forms both of cinema and of other arts, and his sense of the constantly developing interrelations of art, history, literature, and science. Only this can give him an awareness of the possibilities of the cinema, because the cinema is a medium distilled out of previous modes of expression synthesized by science. Yet, so far, only a tiny segment of India lives in the scientific ambience of the twentieth century; the rest is one enormous anachronism struggling to leap into the present.

Those of us who would like to see Indian cinema on the sophisticated level of films from the West (or Japan) tend to forget that the forces weighing down Indian cinema are special and massive. Even the most avant-garde section of the Indian film industry is still subject to crushing pressures—from both past and present.

The absorption of the twentieth-century medium of the cinema, born and developed in industrially advanced countries, into India's classical and folk culture presents enormous problems. India is one country, but has over 800 'mother-tongues'; 16 languages with scripts of their own are recognized in the

Constitution; the diversity in religions, races, costumes, customs, food habits, looks and outlooks, cultural backgrounds is greater than within the entirety of Western civilization. The advanced middle class is one of the most sophisticated in the world. But some tribal people still live in the neolithic age; other groups exist, as it were, in medieval times. Even the educated, once inside their homes, often go back centuries, leaving the modern world in the office and the drawing room; they use the products of science without allowing science itself to penetrate their beings and change the structure of their minds. In India the industrial revolution began barely twenty years ago; neither its pace nor its influence is yet adequate to give the cinema—a product of science and technology—a sense of belonging to the times. Yet now some 800 or so full-length features are produced and released in India and abroad by 61 studios, 39 laboratories, 1,000 producers, and 1,200 distributors; films were shown in 6,000-odd theatres to an audience of more than two billion a year—the fourth largest in the world. There are films for nationwide or 'all-India' distribution made in Bombay and Madras (in Hindi or its variant Hindustani) and there are regional films made in many states —of which the most numerous are the Bengali, well-known for Satyajit Ray.

For more than a century, progress in India has been the outcome of a successful synthesis of Indian tradition with a Western education in the sciences and the humanities. But this culture, brought about by Tagore, Gandhi, and Nehru, is the culture of the advanced middle class; it still leaves out the overwhelming majority of the population to whom the twentieth century and its products are only a necessary evil to be lamented. In the popular mind, you resist this *kaliyuga* by mentally withholding yourself from its contamination or you are corrupted and fall from grace as defined by tradition.

Even the railway train and the radio are still unconnected facts—things that exist and must be used, but without any consciousness of where they came from or how. Science has only confused the Indian villager's philosophy and his pattern of living. The products of science have only brought vulgarity into his existence. This lack of integration between the disparate aspects of life is a constant source of vulgarity in social manifestations and in so-called cultural phenomena—the vulgarity of synthetic, folksy art, of the garish painting of ancient temples, of the harshness of naked fluorescent tube lights, of the sons of five-year-plan contractors playing transistors under massive banyan trees, of dignified old peasants breaking into an ugly trot to cross city streets.

With Independence came the stimulation of industrial growth, the opening up of communications (without a corresponding broadening of education), population pressures, rising prices : these ugly features of a colonial subcivilization have, instead of diminishing, multiplied themselves. Independence has lifted the cultural disciplines of anti-British politics and let loose many disparate cultural tendencies. The cultural leadership of the country has been too inadequate to bring to the masses the same synthesis between East and West which people like Tagore and Nehru brought to the advanced middle class. The failure to absorb the cinema into the Indian tradition is only a part of this larger failure.

Yet the breakdown of folk culture, the rise of an uneducated industrial working class coming into money, of middlemen who thrive on government spending, the increasing outward conformity of the nouveaux riches to a vulgar pseudo-Western pattern (in the absence of any other pattern), the increased mixing between men and women—all this has created the need for an entertainment formula that can cater to an increasingly common set of denominators.

The Hindi (i.e., all-India) film formula not only caters to these denominators, but also helps to create and consolidate them, giving its public certain terms of reference for its cultural adjustment, no matter how low the level of that culture and adjustment may be. It thus supplies a kind of cultural leadership, and reinforces some of the unifying tendencies in our social and economic changes. It provides an inferior alternative to the valid cultural leadership which has not emerged because of the hiatus between the intelligentsia, to which the leaders belong, and the masses—many of them living in remote corners of the country. One cold spring morning in Manali (7,000 feet up in the northwestern foothills of the Himalayas)

I heard a woman's voice softly singing a Hindi film song out-side my window. I went out to investigate and met a family which crosses the 14,000-foot Rohtang Pass every spring, from Lahaul Valley on the Tibet border, to seek work on this side. Every spring they go to Kulu to the cinema there, and the wife was singing a song from a film she had seen the previous year. For her, the experience of a Hindi film once a year was a tiny window on the world beyond the Rohtang Pass.

The basic ingredients in the all-India film for the labourer from Lahaul as well as the half-educated petty bourgeois com-prise not only an operatic assembly of all possible spectacles, sentiments, melodrama, music and dancing, but a mix of these calculated to appeal to the righteous inertia of the audience. In the absence of any other explanation of technological phe-nomena, it is the Hindi film which holds forth : 'Look at the Twentieth Century, full of night clubs and drinking, smoking, bikini-clad women sinfully enjoying themselves in fast cars and mixed parties; how right you are in condemning them— in the end everyone must go back to the traditional patterns of devotion to God, to parents, to village life, or be damned forever.' This answer does not try to explain; it merely echoes the natural fear which traditional people have of anything new, anything they do not understand. The films thus give reassurance to the 'family audience' which is the mainstay of the film industry. They pander to the puritanism developed in the dark pre-British period of superstition and isolationism, aided and abetted by Christian missionary teaching of the British period. They satisfy the common man's curiosity re-garding the ways of the new times but do not explain them. They not only do not try to make him think; they do everything possible to stop him from thinking. Film landscapes change weirdly from Bombay to Tokyo or Delhi to Honolulu, air-planes land and big cars whiz past; the story has no logic, but the songs are delectable, the heroines glamorous, the dances carry the viewer off his feet. Yet in the end he has not sinned himself; like the Code-supervised American moviegoer of yore, he has merely inspected the sins of others before con-demning them. The hero with whom he identifies has re-turned to his true love, the village belle, and renounced the city siren. Sin belongs to the West; virtue to India. Between the two Sharmila Tagores—one a cabaret dancer and the other a demurely Indian damsel—of *Evening in Paris,* no compromise, no middle tones are possible. The more the nouveaux riches rock and roll or twist and shake in blue jeans, the deeper becomes the schizophrenia between modernity and tradition in the Indian cinema. The all-India film thus paradoxically becomes the most effective obstacle against the development of a positive attitude towards technological progress, towards a synthesis of tradition with modernity for a future pattern of living.

If India's course today is still being guided by the Tagore-Nehru dream of an East-West synthesis, the all-India film actively prevents the filtering down of that dream from the advanced middle class to the wider base of the population. It is thus a conformist, reactionary film, out to prevent social revolution rather than to encourage it. In this conformism, the censorship helps. You can criticize the prime minister in the Indian press but not in films. Occasionally when we see a corrupt policeman in a film, we are overjoyed by the liberality of the censors. It is impossible in films to go openly against the basic attitudes of the Establishment. Not only in prudery on sex but in hypocrisy on all possible things, the cinema must conform. It therefore undermines the ideas of the Establishment indirectly, but effectively.

The form of this cinema follows its content. In India film has largely been a receptacle for the mixing together of other media, rather than a medium in itself. Today's Hindi cinema lacks no acting talent; but it is not meant to be used. What passes for acting is a game between the producer and the audience played with well-established types—the crying mother, the doting father, the dancing, singing, dewy-eyed heroine, the sad-faced or epileptic hero, the comic, the precocious child—in which a few mannerisms of the actor are enough for the audience to take the details for granted, so that one can proceed quickly to the climax at which someone will burst into song or dance. It is not as if serious acting or storytelling is suddenly interrupted by a song; the 'action' is in fact merely a preparation for the song. Similarly the situations are stock situations, with stock responses too ready-made to require any exploration of why or how something has happened; the sooner the rest of the action springing from a situation (in a night club, a swimming party, a sentimental scene between father and daughter) can be taken for granted, the better. The films are long, as folk entertainment has always been; the opposition between good and evil is sharp, as it has always been in the epics and legends. Some of the traditional characteristics of folk entertainment have been cleverly exploited to promote the opposite of the harmony with the environment which such entertainment achieved.

Today the songs are competently written, composed, and sung, as in *Sangam*—at intolerably high pitch for my ears but loudly enough to reach up to the Lahaul Valley; the dances are smartly executed, as in *Anita ;* the girls are pretty (too many to name); the colour is good, the sets well-designed, as in *Palki*; the locations well-selected (*Sangam*); the fights convincing, as in *Ganga Jumna;* the censor-deceiving sex-appeal cunningly contrived (*Anita*). The Hindi cinema has not only produced a pop culture, but pop songs which are comparable in rhythm, melody, and verve to those of any country : an effective concoction made of borrowings from classical and folk backgrounds, even Tagore songs and Western music. The dancing is similarly culled from all conceivable styles but gells into the sprightly form of Vaijayanthimala, leaving no dull moment to be dedicated to thought. But in spite of its competence and its verve, it is neither Indian, nor cinema.

Yet with the erosion of the traditional forms of folk entertainment and the trek into the cities in search of employment, this cinema (in the absence of television) quickly established itself as the only diversion of the public—fulfilling its diverse needs for drama, music, farce, dancing, escape into illusions of high living, into fantastic dreams of sin and modernity from which to return to the daily grind.

The sixties found the Hindi cinema spiralling up in costs as it expanded in spectacle; diseases which had been inherent in the system since the war broke out into a first-class crisis when 60 out of 70 Bombay films, each costing over half a million dollars, failed at the box office in 1967. Well over 60 per cent of the production costs went to meet the fees of the stars. With each star acting in several films at the same time, the annual income of some of them (in a country with an average per capita income of some Rs. 600 a year) is higher than that of the top Hollywood stars. Since the money is 'black' and mostly paid under the counter, the Indian star's income-tax worries are rather less than those of his Hollywood counterpart. No wonder the films which are so aptly described by journalists as the 'vehicles' of these stars are unreal from start to finish.

'Black money' originated during the scarcities of the wartime years, when the spoils of large-scale profiteering stayed outside the banks; it has remained there ever since. An industry which costs more in services than in goods offered an excellent area for this unaccounted and untaxed wealth to hide and multiply. The moneybags offered fantastic sums to the stars to wean them away from the studios, which were soon forced to close down. Since then, Indian production has been completely 'independent' everywhere except the South. 'Independents' dependent on stars are hardly likely to be able to hold their own against them. Now the inevitable has happened. The economics of the blockbuster have over-reached the economic potential of the single formula, however perfect. In imitating Hollywood, the mass film in India has landed itself in a star system without studio control, formula filmmaking without Hollywood's variety of formulas, an annual investment of some 85 million dollars without Hollywood's audience research or other organizational safeguards.

The trouble with the Hindi cinema is not that it is commercial; all film industries in the world, including the state-owned ones, are commercial because they cannot go on throwing away money on films which people do not want to see. The trouble is that other film industries do two things that the Hindi cinema does not (for the simple reason that it is incapable) : produce films at many levels ranging from pure art to pure commerce, and occasionally bowl over the art critic and the box office with the same film. Diligently, the Hindi cinema has perfected its one and only formula. It has had no John Ford turning out Westerns, no Milestone making memorable war films, no Hitchcock to hold us in thrall, no Minnelli, no Donen to make it by music alone. It has no genres. It is impossible to make, in our national cinema, anything like *Judgement at Nuremberg* or *Advise and Consent* or *The Best Man*, although our guru has been Hollywood. It makes no adult films for the literate middle class. It is idle to draw much comfort from Basu Bhattacharya's *Teesri Kasam* or *Uski Kahani* or Hrishikesh Mukherjee's *Anupama ;* in any case these films are significant *only* in the context of the Hindi cinema. All that they mean in the end is the reappearance of some sort of middle-class film on the Hindi market. Even with the fullest freedom, what was the net achievement of such stalwart directors as Shantaram or Bimal Roy ? Shantaram had some honest intentions, some cinematic gimmicks wrapped up in execrable taste; his *Jhanak Jhanak* and *Shakuntala* have done as much harm to Indian cinema as Ravi Varma's naturalism did to Indian painting. Bimal Roy, except in the first half of *Do Bigha Zamin* stayed with melodrama and sentimentality in slightly better taste. In Raj Kapoor's *Sangam* the audience is asked to believe that two adult men, whose dedication to friendship is almost pathological, take twenty reels to find out that they are in love with the same girl. Traditionally, narrative literature has asked for the suspension of disbelief; the Kapoorian phantasmagoria demands the total surrender of the rational part of man, leaving the animal staring dumbly at helicopters and locations in Europe. The problem is not one of freedom; it is one of cynicism, ignorance, and cultural underdevelopment. That is why, when it decides to be good or tries to be 'art', Hindi cinema is dreadfully self-conscious, didactic, and pretentious.

The regional film, as we shall see, has its roots, its sense of identity; it tends to underplay the common factors arising in the country and stresses elements of regional tradition with some pride and nostalgia. In the all-India film, no male character except the villain can wear Indian costume; in the regional film almost the opposite is true. The regional film likewise shows more of rural and urban lower-middle-class life. The all-India film, anxious to avoid pronouncedly regional characteristics in its search for wide acceptability, avoids these and weaves its fancies round high-income brackets where Westernized uniformity is more easily available. There is thus a greater sense of reality and cultural integrity in the regional film; it is Indian, even when it is not cinema. Its main concerns are with social problems, as in literature.

The position was much the same with the Hindi film until the war. In the days of Bombay talkies and films like *Achut Kanya* or *Jivan Prabhat*, the attitudes of the Bombay film (or the Madras Hindi film) and the Bengali film from Calcutta were more or less the same. They shared the social reformist zeal of the advanced middle class of those times, as much as literature or journalism. The evils of caste, the right to love before marriage, the tragic taboo against widow remarriage, ideas of individualism, secularism, and democracy provided the subject matter of most films whether in regional languages or in Hindi. The form was by no means cinematic but the content was definitely Indian. It was much closer to the ideals of the country's leadership than today.

The shortages of the war not only brought about 'black money', high star fees, and the end of studio production, but initiated a profound change in the character of the audience of the Hindi cinema. With the wartime emphasis on production began the rise of the industrial working class. In independent India the process was further emphasized with labour legislation and encouragement of trade unionism. But industry made progress out of all proportion to education, whose standards have in fact declined with the population pressure. In comparison to the landless labourer whose name is legion, the industrial working class became a privileged minority. In this it became bracketed with other nouveau riche sections of society, such as those that bag the contracts and subcontracts of the massive five-year plans. To these were added, in the sixties, the dealers in food grains and the big and the middle farmers who made killings during the food shortages. In other words, the Hindi cinema after the war found itself forced to address its appeal to a culturally impoverished nouveau riche audience, increasingly disoriented from the cultural ambitions of new India and falling back on a schizophrenic solution of being extremely conservative inside and outwardly ultramodern.

The educated minority in the Hindi-speaking areas accepted this cinema as much as the masses, in the absence of an alternative. With this change in the nature of the audience, the Hindi cinema emerged as the all-India cinema by virtue of the position of Hindi as the lingua franca of the country; and the get-rich-quick financiers turned away from social zeal to a cynical-conformist formula of Westernized sin-parade ending in the triumph of tradition.

Inevitably, due to the economics of scale and the spread of new 'all-India' denominators, the regional cinemas receded before the impact of the Hindi film. Colour filming has become virtually impossible in Bengal, for instance. Even Satyajit Ray was forced to drop his colour plans and make his delightful *Goopi Gain Bagha Bain* (based on a fantasy by his grandfather) in black and white. But the film audience in Bengal has remained basically middle class and is by and large educated. This is more or less true of all regional cinemas, and gives them greater artistic potential than the all-India field, as we have seen in the breakthrough of Satyajit Ray, who reflected a resolution of our cultural dilemmas not in terms of its lowest common denominators, but its highest. Ray translated the value world of Tagore into the content and technique of advanced cinema and tried to extend it to contemporary, post-Tagore situations as well. This he was able to do with success, not because the Western world could recognize in it the signposts of India's evolution into the modern world, but because he was able to attract an audience—a fairly sophisticated middle-class audience—on his home ground in Bengal. Here was the Tagore-Nehru dream of a new Indian identity—enshrined in the laws and official goals of the country yet repudiated by the mass cinema—at its best.

But Ray's position in India is not just unique; it is one of splendid isolation. Although his genius is recognized not only by intellectuals but by the average audience in Bengal and by the film industry all over the country, his influence, in relation to his reputation, must be considered negligible. In a characteristically Indian way, film-makers have put him on a pedestal for admiration from a safe distance. He is an exception, a phenomenon, an object of pride for India like the Konarak temple or Banaras textiles. Film-makers think of modelling their work on his no more than they think of building a Taj Mahal to live in. The juggernaut of Indian cinema grinds on.

The Marathi cinema, the only other considerable regional cinema outside the South, was fatally weakened by the expanding Hindi film audience; if it still exists today, it is not due to its inherent strength but to governmental oxygen which keeps it breathing.

It is only at the level of art that the regional film can survive, as the Bengali film has done so far. If Satyajit Ray and other new film-makers did not emerge, the Bengali film would go the way of the Marathi. The only other and somewhat doubtful prescription, which is being tried by some today, is to rouse regional passions and summon them to the aid of the local film. Even this, like the governmental rescue operation, can at best be temporary and partial aid in the recovery. The average Bengali, or any other regional film imitating the all-India pattern or being nostalgic in a heavy-handed, namby-pamby way, is becoming as unbearable to the average audience as it has always been to the sophisticated. In fact the Bengali film enjoys an undeservedly high reputation because of a few artistic successes; the average Bengali film remains a dreadfully dull opiate for a sleepy middle class. For the more contemporary-minded viewer, some films do keep appearing which reflect his restlessness, but the difference between these and the rest seems unbridgeable. The films of Ritwik Ghatak, who died after making only eight feature films, Mrinal Sen, whose *Akash Kusum* was a box-office failure and made him seek distinction in Oriya in his brilliant *Matira Manisha,* not to speak of Satyajit Ray who made an unbroken series of masterpiece and near-masterpieces up to *Charulata,* are far removed from the average Bengali product. Directors like Tapan Sinha and Tarun Majumdar (also to some extent Arup Guha Thakurta and Hari Sadhan Das Gupta) have brought good taste and competent storytelling to present-day Bengali cinema, whereas others have faded away after brief spells of 'experiment' whose purpose has in some cases been vague even to themselves—notably Rajen Tarafder in *Ganga,* Barin Saha in *Tero Nadir Parey,* Purnendu Patrea in *Swapna*

Niye. Pushed to the wall, the Bengali cinema is fighting back hard, trying to find in box office-cum-art what it cannot in terms of the lavishness and sprightliness of Hindi film. In Tarun Majumdar's *Balika Bodhu* or Arundhati Devi's *Chhuti* it has absorbed something of the creative techniques of Ray, Ghatak and Sen, and turned it into the routine of mediocre poets and the stuff of the box office. The leadership of culture which lay for some ten years in the domain of the cinema is fast moving into the amateur theatre, which now provides greater freedom to the artist.

The states of Assam and Orissa have not yet done too much to save themselves from the future pressures of the all-India film either in terms of solid box-office foundations or the escape route of art. The Oriya audience completely rejected Mrinal Sen's *Matira Manisha*—imaginative, sensitively photographed and acted, and directed with a big heart—because it does not conform to its source, a novel; obviously the Oriyas are not yet ready for the sophistications of the film medium, and must stick to the copy book of the filmed theatre. I have no doubt that they will rediscover the film after some years of industrial development.

Madras made its dent into Bombay's monopoly of the Hindi market as early as 1948 with S. S. Vasan's *Chandralekha*. Although South India provides a large enough audience to sustain a regional cinema, it has made regular forays outside its natural boundaries and Southern films still appear on the all-India screen. The 'common' factors are developing here, too, enabling many Tamil films to come out in Hindi versions to compete—often successfully—with the all-India film. The fact that South India has something of a unity of its own, despite the existence of many languages, has given its regional film a wider audience than the Oriya, Assamese, or Bengali film whose audience is virtually confined to its own linguistic area. Telugu actors appear often in Tamil, Malayalam films get easily shown in Madras, the Kannada film is more easily understood in Andhra than is the case with films in the North Indian languages. Binding them together, however, is the formula of song-dance-melodrama in which reality is of little consequence. This formula precludes the cinema of narrative illusion; it is unabashed spectacle, vulgarized but closer to traditions of popular variety shows than to literature or drama. Even its music and dance are breaking out of the tradition of the Carnatic system and picking up the postures of the Hindi cinema of Bombay. It is only in superficialities that it maintains some semblance of regionalism.

There have been minor exceptions to this; D. Jayakanthan has shown a superior sensibility for literary-dramatic values (more than cinematic ones) in *Unnaipol Oruvan*. The Malayalam cinema, always of a more literary nature than the Tamil, has thrown up over-rated, but above-the-local-average films like *Neelakuvil,* jointly directed by Ramu Kariat and P. Bhaskaran, on untouchability and unmarried motherhood. The Malayalam cinema, like the Bengali and Marathi, has remained occupied with social problems—a concern which the Tamil cinema abandoned long ago in order to catch up with the all-India box office. The work of the mildly interesting South Indian directors has sometimes been praised beyond all proportion because of its rarity and because of the general lack of understanding of the film medium or its achievements in other countries and periods. The malaise here is worse than the hero worship of the late P. C. Barua in Bengal and of Shantaram in Maharashtra as geniuses of the cinema—as if their work was comparable to that of Eisenstein or Dreyer, Ford or Renoir.

The fact is that although some of these directors and films have borne a slight stamp of individuality, an ardour for a good cause, snatches of realism and touches of cinema, even some emotional power within their own notions of drama, they never really left the framework of the filmed theatre and the variety show; at best they groped towards the language of the cinema. Discussing nine South Indian social films of 1964 which received regional awards from the Government of India, S. Krishnaswamy wrote : 'In nearly all the nine films, the climax is developed with illness, death or accident. Five have hospital scenes, one has a scene of chronic illness building up to a climax, and the three others feature suicide, murder and death by accident. The doctor is a favorite character. Disputes are resolved by offering blood to the dying, sympathy created by being in bed.'

Of the background music he says : 'You hear the same set of notes in similar situations on the screen, as though a common track is used from a music library.' And finally of D. Jayakanthan's *Unnaipol Oruvan*: 'It is conceived more as a drama than as a screenplay. It conveys less by vision than by words. Except for one, the performances are superb, the material surroundings are much less convincing than the people themselves. The art direction is unimaginative, photography uneven, and editing poorly conceived . . . Jayakanthan has not produced an outstanding film, but it is a milestone in southern film history.' ('Madras Letter', *Indian Film Culture,* No. 6.)

I believe that in terms of box-office economics, the fate of the regional film, perhaps sooner elsewhere than in the South, is sealed. It is only in terms of art that the Bengali cinema, the Oriya or the Assamese, or the newly identity-proud Gujarati and Konkani film, will survive in the end, bolstered up by state finances or art theatres or whatever mechanics we eventually arrive at for making it possible to have artistic films for a minority audience. (In a country like India, even a minority is large enough to contend with—it may surpass the population of Scandinavia.)

And there is no doubt that a minority audience is fast coming into being, thanks to the international film festivals, film societies, film institutes, formidable new forces in the documentary (which has thrown up a number of good films in the last three years), film archives, serious film magazines, state recognition for good films, state finance, and a wider spread of import sources. These forces, despite occasional signs of defeat, are in fact gathering some strength; more people are beginning to get a taste of real cinema and becoming impatient to try their hand at the medium, to hold their doors wide open to influences and examples from all over the world. Their dissatisfactions and creative urges are bound to find expression, sooner or later, in a kind of cinema which may or may not cater to the vast populace, but will find sufficient buyers to break out into art theatres and the film-club circuit (now consisting of about a hundred groups). Under its pressures, even the commercial cinema may have to undergo at least superficial changes in form, although perhaps not in spirit. The trail blazed by the Bengalis is already being followed by other regions who might also find paths of their own; and the total impact of India's regional films—like the best of the Bengali—may yet be memorable in world cinema.

1968

in defence of the
box office

It is probably due to the situation in the other arts, through which one arrives at the cinema, that the notion of the separateness of the film as an art and as box office has gained ground and assumed an air of finality. The fact that films, unlike painting, music or poetry, cannot be produced without reference to a wide public, has been the subject of some remorse. No less a person than Jean Renoir expressed the hope that television would some day take over all that is cheap in the cinema and leave it a pure art. Yet Renoir himself is one of those very few artists in the cinema who has wrested a universality and significance out of the box office that is somewhat rare today in the other 'purer' arts. Is it a disadvantage for the artist that the cinema, by insisting on universality, presents a fatal choice between cheapness and greatness ?

Universality has always been the ideal condition of art; in the cinema it is the only condition and, therefore, presents the greatest challenge to an artist. Here no ivory towers can be built; the box office sees to that. If communication is the basis of all art, the box office guards that basis by ruling out the private gesture, the purely personal complex. It is the cinema's guarantee of universality : that is why the cinema was born, in answer to the needs of our age for a widely communicative art, at a time when the other arts had retired from that necessary service to the public. The mantle of greatness has fallen on the cinema today much as it fell on the epic in ancient times or on the drama in the Elizabethan age. Should it (and can it) be shaken off and put round the shoulders of television ?

The condition of greatness being also the condition of cheapness, the cinema must produce much that is cheap. Indeed, no other art produces as much cheapness today. The typical art of any age has its appeal at various levels and contains much that is popular merely because it is cheap. Renoir himself once pointed out that the world has always produced more bad books than good books—even in the age of Shakespeare. But the cinema also yields a good deal of what is artistically valid and universally popular at the same time and thus approaches the highest condition of any art. In little more than half a century of its existence, the cinema has perhaps offered more universal classics than all the other arts taken together during this period. With what literary masterpiece of this century would you compare *The Gold Rush* ?

The cinema's need to be universally understood is fully realised by its practitioners. After all, nobody makes a film so that it should be a box office failure. On the other hand, the best films are not those that have best swept the box office. The problem has been, therefore, to make a virtue rather than a vice of the necessity to be popular. Only through greatness has such virtue been achieved. In the cinema, it should not be embarrassing to talk of greatness even if people have been slow to recognise it because it is so contemporary. Everyone knows that Chaplin found his way to the heart of the audience in the struggle between the big man and the little man which he portrayed. He chose the most basic problem of our age for his content and gave it the form of a most basic humour. The horseplay was always broad enough for the lowest common denomination of intelligence; even the sentimental streak was the perfectly bourgeois accompaniment to it. It was into the lowest vaudeville horseplay that he put the greatest significance. In doing so, he created a humour which expressed its meaning, like all great art, at various levels. Shakespeare produced *Hamlet* because the groundlings wanted bloody murder. Chaplin produced *The Gold Rush* because the audience liked slapstick, surrendering his artistic integrity no more than Shakespeare did. The American cinema, the widest target of critical gunfire, has probably produced the steadiest stream of classic films in the long span from *Intolerance* to *Friendly Persuasion*.

Take the Western tradition, a peculiar product of the American cinema, pioneered by no less a person than John Ford. Here, not only the work of an individual but an entire, important genre in the American cinema is built on a deeply based myth. The success of the Western lies in its symbolization of the growth of a country and a civilization. It is a symbolism that is deeply felt in the United States and because of its profound regional truth, is understood outside the United States too. The spirit of struggle and adventure to which it appeals is universal. Man grapples with the earth and makes it yield; where there was desolation there is now a city—that is the essential message of the Western tradition presented in the simplest terms of virile action and beautiful landscape. The poetry of the Western is never altogether lost even in its worst examples, which is why one would rather see a bad Western than a bad social film, if the choice lay between the two. Flaherty, too, found his answer in portraying 'man against the sky' in a simple and childlike manner. It is said that since its appearance in 1921, *Nanook* has been showing somewhere or the other in the world every week.

Altogether, the incidence of art in the box office has probably been higher in Hollywood than in any other film industry over a comparable period. Short-lived spells have overtaken other film industries from time to time, yielding no lesser results. The great period of Russian cinema was inspired by a universally understood sense of triumph, and a hope for the future; the French cinema of Renoir and Carné by its spirit of exploration of real life. In the British wartime renaissance, the idea of documentary truth became emotionalized by the tension of war in a peculiarly British way of understatement, of silent heroism. In the postwar period Italy expressed the new concern for common man which came in the wake of devastation. In all these countries, in the best examples of the basic trend during these periods of flowering, the problem of the box office was somehow solved because the artists sought to express something that was of importance to the world and could not be confined to any group of people initiated in the mysteries of an esoteric art. Never did those who put the blame on the audience when their films fail to move it, create any better. It is not time yet in India to talk of a trend, a myth or an idea on which a body of universal films have been made. Yet at least one outstanding example of the success of art in the box office has been seen—in *Pather Panchali*.

The one lesson which emerges from all this, to my mind, is the fact that an 'artistic' film succeeds in the box office only when an artist goes down on his knees to the audience so that he cannot look down upon it. It is idle to blame the audience. The fault, dear Brutus, is in ourselves. Because he must please, not just himself, or his friends but millions, a filmmaker, more than any other artist, needs humility. The starting point must be, not one's own mind, but that of the audience. Then begins one's deep search for a relation to it. Instead of fighting the box office the artist might as well accept it as the guardian of his health. For it is he who needs defence; the box office needs none.

We in the East have no reason to be embarrassed by the idea of the challenge of 'greatness'. For a variety of reasons, reflections on the cinema in the West have been forced back upon a frustrated acceptance of a division between art and box office. There have been too many frustrations; there are too few widely accepted and inspiring faiths to provide a positive basis of communication. Besides, it is not respectable in the other arts to believe in universal communication and the film, alas, is still in such need of respectability that there is a chorus of protest at Lindsay Anderson's 'Stand Up! Stand Up!' (*Sight & Sound*). That article, however, takes a very humanist, deliberately 'socially conscious' standpoint which has aroused controversies in all other arts before and takes no note of the special condition of the cinema, which does not license the construction of expensive ivory towers. In the East where the film medium is yet to come into its own, the horizon is so wide, the air so charged with possibilities, that scepticism is much less natural, unless it is borrowed from abroad as a fashionable attitude. The time for scepticism may come after the fate of Britain and Italy, Russia and France has also overtaken the Japanese film, or the Indian; the time is certainly not now. Also, in the awakening of Asia, there is a strong element of faith in the future, a basis for inspiration. And these are not the sole advantages either. The vast unlettered audiences of the East are yet a long way from acquiring the bourgeois prejudices; the middle class is yet too small for that. It is only the urban middle class which, in India, will question the distortions of the human figure in painting, for example. The villager has long been used to folk art which has no more respect for the outward features of the human physiognomy than 'modern' painting. He has enough simplicity to believe and to accept the beauty of line and colour. The average Indian villager will put a daily garland round the painting of a hydra-headed, multi-handed and thoroughly flattened and distorted god which would be inconceivable for a British coal miner or an American cotton picker to accept in the most religious picture. That the same Indian will accept with equal reverence a crude example of mythological art on a commercial calendar is another matter, due to another set of reasons, which does not affect the issue. On seeing a head by Jamini Roy a villager who had come to town for the first time said : 'It looks exactly like a photograph !'

How is this an advantage ? Obviously, to such an audience, the content means more than the form and there are few preconceived notions or acquired prejudices to prevent a simple reaction to an essential expression. Also, there is less of a search for mere novelty and sensation which is bred by high pressure existence. Because the content is so well-known to the audience, the artist has the greatest freedom with the form. Take the legend of Radha and Krishna. The story is fully known to the audience. Yet, for many centuries the same story has served as an enormous canvas which generations of artists have filled in and coloured with layers and layers of personal expression, building levels upon levels of meaning. On it has thrived the poetry of the mystics, the four main classical dances, the *Kirtan* and many other musical forms, a great section of traditional painting including such delicate styles as Kangra. The legend is almost as great as life itself; it encompasses the whole range of basic human emotions, desires, philosophic thought, character, spectacle. A man may take from it what he wants. It is like the sea receiving countless rivers into itself. Children may delight in Krishna stealing the butter; youths in Krishna stealing the clothes of maidens bathing in a stream; white-haired widows may find bliss in the symbolism of complete dedication to the deity. Sexual love, described in pages upon pages of exquisite sensuality is so inextricably entwined with the sentimental as well as philosophic love of God, that the whole complex scale of the feeling and concept of love is built up with perfect fluency. It is impossible to find the dividing line where God ends and the beloved begins.

Discourses on politics and philosophy are rampant in the Mahabharata whose story is as rich in metamorphoses as Ovid's and as full of resounding battles as Homer's. Krishna, the motivator of the Mahabharata, is considered an incarnation of God in the more traditional spiritual approach; yet he may be sketched as a Machiavelli by a materialist, for most of his actions are a pursuit of good ends through bad means. So un-Gandhian in his actions, Krishna's philosophy was the guiding spirit of Gandhiji's life and work. Innumerable contradictions make up the monumental canvas of the Krishna myth. Its very completeness assures the resolution of all personal problems with their endless variety. Yet serve it in any form, and as long as the outline is recognisable, there is complete acceptance. In Orissa, intricately stylized folk paintings of the Krishna legend are still painted in hundreds and sold in the local market for a few paise a piece; yet the mythological film, the very worst expression of Indian cinema in every possible manner, has a guaranteed success in Orissa as much as in any other part of India. Such a situation would strike the Western mind as a quaint museum piece. Yet the situation obtains in India today and tradition lives. The epics and legends are deeply embedded in the minds of even the sophisticated audience. And the masses of the people will accept a variation in artistic *form* to an extent that Western audiences would not dream of accepting in a Christian legend. As for the content, it is as if the Greek pantheon was real and alive to the entire people of Europe today.

The opportunity this provides to the Indian film-maker is massive. Here is all the scope for experimentation with form, for turning the medium inside out, with the least risk. The artist, like the box-office tycoon, can 'Give 'em what they want' and yet do what he wants to do. The trick photography in our mythologicals delights the audience. Is it an enemy of art? The Cocteau of *La Belle et la bete* would not have thought so. What would Eisenstein have made of the battle of Kurukshetra? He would not have been embarrassed by the vastness of the spectacle. The moral content would not be spurned by philosophers either. Take the example of Yudhisthira's encounter with the god Dharma (virtue). The five brothers have roamed in the forest all day and are thirsty and tired. One by one they go to fetch water. Each comes upon a pond in the forest and as he is about to drink, is challenged by a crane and asked to answer some questions before he drinks. All the four disregard the challenge and perish, for the crane is Dharma himself, in disguise. Finally Yudhisthira, the eldest and noblest of the Pandavas, comes to the edge of the water. The first four questions asked are:

Crane : What is the message of life ?

Yudhisthira : The world is the cauldron in which all beings lie; the sun is the fuel; the months and the seasons are the ladle; and the hand that cooks it all is that of Time. That is the message of life.

Crane : What is the wonder of life ?

Yudhisthira : That every hour numberless beings enter the temple of Death; yet those who remain want to live for ever.

Crane : Who is the happy man ?

Yudhisthira : Happy is the man who is not in debt to anyone, does not live away from his own land, and cooks himself a simple meal at the end of the day.

Crane : What is the path ?

Yudhisthira : The Vedas say one thing, the Smritis another; there is not one thinker whose thought is not different from the other's. The secret of virtue lies ever hidden from us. The only path is the one that great men before us have walked.

Dharma, pleased with the answers, now leaves the guise of the crane and reveals himself. He asks Yudhisthira again: 'I will now revive one of your brothers; tell me, which one will it be?' Yudhisthira names his youngest stepbrother. 'Why,' asks Dharma, 'why not the great hero Arjuna or the mighty Bhima, who are your own brothers?' 'So that my stepmother also should have a son alive, for my mother has me,' says Yudhisthira. Dharma now revives all of them, for Yudhisthira has passed the test. The five brothers are re-united.

A simple story which brings together the supernatural and the spectacular with the ethics and philosophy of man.

The myths are so great that they are capable of countless interpretations. Overtones of contemporary feeling may envelope them (think of Kurosawa). In India, mythology often borders on history, social history at any rate, and history in the scientific sense has been somewhat at a discount. Hence, the renewed material consciousness of today can find inspiration in the mythological tales. There are examples of folk dancing and singing, such as the Gambhira in West Bengal, which feature contemporary problems within the framework of mythology. One basic idea in the present resurgence of India is that it is the re-assertion of an ancient civilization, re-oriented to the problems of the present. The most 'progressive' Indian is today engaged in a rediscovery of his own country, on which he had once turned his back under the influence of his Western education. The deeper the Western education has been, the stronger is now the urge for this rediscovery.

Slowly, the mythological tales are acquiring a new meaning under this searching light. Instead of hanging in the void, they are gradually becoming related to social history and their origins and intentions are beginning to be understood. In the variety of their levels of appeal, their tacit acceptance by the masses and their renewed, if limited, understanding by the more sophisticated, in their expression of the 'spirit of India', as it were, the epics and myths of the country would seem to present the most widely acceptable base for the artistic development of the Indian cinema. (Needless to say, such a development will borrow little from the present run of 'mytholo-

gicals' !) The artist may find here a fundamental relationship with his audience; he can explore the depths of the
medium in his search for its essence; he can express his personal emotions and involve those of the audience without
leaving his concern for form for a moment. By accepting the
lowest common basis of knowledge, taste and faith in an
audience of tremendous variety, he is no longer in opposition
to it but carries it along with him. In other subjects there is
the exciting possibility of making fine individual films which
the box office may accept or reject. Here there is an opportunity to build an artistic tradition on the box office itself.

This must sound like a very personal solution. It is. It is
impossible to press it as the general solution to all problems
and to rule out all other ways by which the artist might make
peace with his audience. Yet, one might be permitted one
generalization; you need a myth of some kind, and it had
better be a big one. It must have the maximum possibility
of wide acceptance. To an extent it is true that most films
create, or try to create, a myth of some kind. But that is too
slender a basis on which to bring together art and the box
office. What one needs is an easily understood, well-known
outline which can be filled by film after film, artist after artist.

Another generalization : We must accept the audience as it
is. Among the progressive film-makers, there are too many
preconceived notions derived from the form of the film as
seen in the West. To the masses that make the audience
for Hindi films, songs seem to be of great importance. To
us they seem to hold up the story; to them the story is incomplete without them. Suppose, for a change, one tries to understand this phenomenon instead of railing against it. The
fact that the sources of popular music outside the cinema have
dried up is not the only reason. Perhaps the story is not of
as much importance to them as it is to us. Even today a
classical music session lasts the whole night; people go out
to stretch their legs, eat potato chips, exchange gossip, coming
back to the music every now and then. That is more true of
folk dances or folk singing, including those which relate stories.
They are not like short stories with beautifully chiselled form,
complete with a beginning, a middle and an end. They are

rather like the epics, which you can read from anywhere to anywhere, as long as you like. There is no need to begin from the beginning and stop at the end, for you know what has gone before, also what is to come. You enjoy the present rather than seek the before or the after. A village woman in Bengal would enjoy a folk play no less because she arrives in the middle; she has seen the play many times before. The same attitude applies to all folk entertainment in India— whether it is singing, dancing, drama, opera. However different it may seem, the same attitude prevails in the Indian film audience. It delights more in the present than in the past or the future. It is more interested in the action itself than in its result. While a song is being sung, *that* is the most important thing; whether the story is held up or not matters little. In the traditional Bengali drama, the *jatra,* the action is interrupted from time to time by a song that, like the Greek chorus, underlines the meaning or the moral of the action. The songs have somehow become part of the form; again, because there is no hurry to find out what happens next. The artist who has understood this tradition may well be able to fashion a form in the cinema which embodies the song as an integral part of the film. The study of the character of tradition in folk entertainment may help in arriving at a form which is not borrowed from the West and imposed on our people but born from the needs of the people themselves.

The two-dimensional, linear quality which distinguishes almost all forms of Indian art may have an influence on the cinema too. Indian painting is mostly flat, without 'perspective'; Indian music melodic, devoid of tonal perspective, harmony or counterpoint; Indian dancing emphasises the flowing line more than anything else; even Indian sculpture is best seen from a given angle. Indian art has never revolted against representation; yet representation has not lowered it. The seated Buddha or the dancing Nataraja are both fully recognisable human figures; yet they are perfect visual expressions of abstract ideas—of meditation in one and movement in the other. The view of life in Indian tradition, unlike the Western, is not a 'tragic' one. Here life is seen as a continuous, unending line, rather than a tightly enclosed pattern of tragic heroism. It is a line of resolution, not of conflict.

Strange as this may seem, it is in this make-up of the Indian mind that the secret to it may lie. The preference is for the epic rather than the dramatic form. All the conventions of the box office point in this direction: the dislike for unpleasant endings; the tolerance of enormous lengths; the lack of sufficient concern for the progress of the story; the comparative insensitivity to the drama of conflict. The film moghuls have fully sensed these traits of the audience without knowing the reasons for them. In answer, they have produced Bradshaws of entertainment, vulgar in taste and low in level but appealing all the same to the man for whom it is meant. They have served up a myth after a fashion and it has worked. The hero may fall in love with the wicked woman from the city ; but he must go back to the innocent village belle in the end and marry her. It is only the recent 'socially conscious', more modern, pseudo-realistic film from Bombay which has no sure hold on the box office. The reason is that it has been inspired by the International Film Festival rather than by tradition and its maker's level of thinking and artistic ability has not been very much higher than that of the potbellied merchants of the 'mythological'.

But if the conscious artist of today seeks to understand his audience and its traditions, accepts them himself and concentrates on a myth which the audience will accept—then he may be laying the basis for transmuting the lowest common level to the highest possible achievement of the Indian cinema—in art as well as in the box office.

1957

music :
opium of the masses ?

Anyone who lives in the heart of Bombay or Calcutta has experience of the multiplicity of music that assails his ears in all his waking hours. Two stations of AIR from the flats above; singing in aid of flood relief on the street; a girl taking music lessons downstairs; shehnai (or a Western band) at a wedding down the block; a blind beggar playing the violin on the pavement; someone practising the sitar somewhere; labourers sounding cymbals and singing community *bhajans*. All this is let loose at the same time, and every sound is at its loudest, expressing an innate need for noise, possibly to obviate the possibility of any thought from occuring at an awkward moment of silence. Background music in Indian films serves the same need for noise—loud noise, and as much of it as possible. Background music is a filler, which gives 'body' to the noise level of the film.

But the issue of film music in India is confused by the fact that most of our films are loaded with songs. Film songs have to satisfy the public's need for popular music because that need is not satisfied through other means. The radio is barely within the reach of the masses; so are gramophones. Folk songs and dances are dying out with the change of the social pattern, and no new forms are taking their place in the life of the people. The impact of Western culture which created an intellectual ferment in the forward sections of the middle class, is being felt more widely and, consequently, at a less intellectual level. There is greater social mixing among men and women, in education and in work, creating the need for new forms of community dancing and singing. In the absence

of evolution of indigenous forms, Western forms or their vul-
garizations catch the imagination of an ever-widening middle
class. And in the absence of other media for the dissemina-
tion of popular music to all classes of people, the cinema is
made to carry this burden since its audience is so large and
widespread. Music thus becomes a menace to the cinema in
a manner which is inconceivable in the West or other industrially developed areas such as Japan. India is one of the
very few countries in the world where every film is a musical.
Whether the theme is realistic or fantastic, social or suspense-
ful, religious or comic, it must be enveloped in songs.

Songs also provide an 'out' for the incompetent film-maker
who is unable to hold the attention of the audience by any
other means. If the average Indian's music-hungry ears could
be filled by music halls, radios in every home, and new forms
of folk songs and light operas, the present Indian film-maker
would find himself in a helpless state. He could no longer
fall back on 'picturized' songs, even using the lowest common
denominator of taste. He would have to make proper films
which please their audience as films and not as 'vehicles' of
songs. This very few have yet learnt to do. Sound came to
our cinema before the silent film had had the opportunity, or
the leadership, to establish the language of the film as a visual
medium. The film is the art of an industrial age, produced
through machines. Its development has, therefore, taken place
in accordance with the industrial development of the country.
It is not surprising, therefore, that it has developed far more
in the West and in Japan, than in underdeveloped economies.
In India it has remained a borrowed form which has not been
integrated with the traditions of the country. It has thus become everything except what it should be—an autonomous
medium of aural-visual expression.

That is why Indian films are overloaded with songs, but
very few are 'musicals' in the Western sense. One would
have imagined that with the Indian's love of music, most of
our films would be 'musicals'. But the cinema in India is burdened with the need, not only to be a vehicle of music, but of
everything that the public wants. No matter how distorted
it may be, the masses do want to see some reflection of their

problems, and of the change that is taking place around them. Where else would they see it except in the cinema—the only medium of popular entertainment ? All films cannot, therefore, be musicals; there must be films on religion to confirm their sense of tradition; on social problems that they grapple with or dimly perceive; on love, to stimulate their sex urge. They are also hungry for stories so some stories must be told. They must be given a picture of the 'modern' society which is novel and exciting to them. They must also have a reflection of the 'rags and riches' contrast of India. Basically most people are fearful of change ; so the hero must in the end marry the village belle who is so good, and renounce the tennis-playing town girl who is so bad. Yet all this must also be made more unreal with a shower of songs, so that they have a taste of everything, without being involved in anything. In this way is born the delectable world of unreality, a fantastic paradise of all possible kinds of entertainment served up in a completely un-Indian, unbelievable form, which has nothing Indian or cinematic about it. In it, music is the opium of the mass audience. And under its influence, the public sees unreal visions of reality, where logic is of little importance, and it does not matter if the story is interrupted every few minutes by a senseless outburst of songs.

The 'pure musical' is, therefore, somewhat rare on the Indian screen. The opium of music is, on the other hand, mixed with every dish that is served up to the audience. Once the audience has acquired the habit, it becomes immensely difficult for a lone man of good intentions to make it taste anything without that essential ingredient. Thus a Tamil director's name has gone down in history because he once made a film without any songs. No one has gone into the merits of the film; the fact that it is without songs, has been sufficient to immortalize its creator—Mr. S. Balachandran. This is not to deny the high quality of some of the lyrics and the tunes which are, in fact, the best thing about the commercial cinema in India, especially in Hindi. With well-known poets like Kaifi Azmi, Shakil Badauni or Majrooh Sultanpuri writing the songs, Sachin Dev Burman, Hemanta Mukherjee, Salil Chowdhury on the one hand, teams like Laxmi-

kant-Pyarelel on the other deriving lilting tunes from every
conceivable source—folk, classical, Western, Rabindrasangeet
et al—no wonder the quality of the film song is often of a
high order. Even the musical accompaniment to a song is
different from background music and much higher in quality.

The Bengali composers I have named earlier are remarkable
for their backgrounds; Sachin Dev Burman was, until he
migrated to Bombay, famous in Bengal as the unique singer
of folk and semi-classical popular songs; Hemanta Mukherjee
began as a remarkable singer of Rabindrasangeet (which he
still sings, but with too much of a microphone-hugging 'croo-
ner' quality); Salil Chowdhury made his mark in the Indian
People's Theatre Association (IPTA) in which Hemanta
Mukherjee had also featured for some time. The achievements of these three in the Hindi cinema are not comparable
to their earlier work in Bengal, and they are often guilty of
plagiarizing from Rabindrasangeet without acknowledgement,
unlike Pankaj Mullick who had sung 'Yaad aye ki na aye' for
New Theatres as a Hindi version of a famous song of Tagore's,
both in tune and words.

The only regional film music of which I can speak with any
certainty is the Bengali. In the days of New Theatres, film
songs often had a sophistication of form and content comparable to the best of Hindi cinema today. With Rabindrasangeet and kirtan in extensive use, Ajoy Bhattacharya turning
out many of the lyrics, K. L. Saigal singing many of the songs,
the standard was often higher. After the fall of New Theatres, the Bengali film song plummetted to the lowest depths
of banality in words, monotony in tunes, and a cloying sentimentality in both. Its only similarity with Bombay is in star
playback singer Sandhya Mukherjee's able imitation of the
high-pitched virtuosity of Lata Mangeshkar. The piercing
quality which Lata, the doyenne of Indian film singing, established as the model for the rest of the country was possibly
derived from the conventions of folk singers who entertained
the populace out in the open without the aid of a microphone.
To this day, itinerant singers in Rajasthan or Madhya Pradesh
travel in couples, the man sporting a rich baritone and the
woman a supersoprano. This convention seems to have been

planted directly into the recording studio with its sensitive microphones and the enclosed cinema theatre with its gigantic speakers.

By unalterable convention, the recordists record, and the theatre projectionists play, the songs at the loudest permitted by their respective machines. Not the slightest compromise in this is tolerated, no matter how pressing the dramatic reason. Thus a heroine coming forward to, or going away from, the camera, will sing in a stationary voice without the slightest tonal perspective. If a voice is supposed to be heard from afar, it will at best be put through an echo device (much abused in all kinds of songs, even when sung inside a small room on the screen), rather than reduce its volume. Time and again, new directors in Bengal have had to persuade recordists to record below the maximum, and to rush up to the projection booth on opening nights to persuade the operator to play the song low (the moment a song comes, he will turn the volume to the loudest, getting back to normal for the other scenes).

The second, and almost as unalterable convention is the one of the playback. A character on the screen must not sing himself; even if he can, it is not politic to upset the playback singer. There are not, and must not be, any singing stars, anymore. World cinema knows the technique of the artist being photographed miming a previously recorded sound track of his own voice; in rare instances, a good singer will 'dub' the voice for a good actor who can't sing. Not so in India. The institution of the playback singer supplying the artist's voice the moment he breaks into song, is a hallowed one, above all questions on counts of mere realism. Lata Mangeshkar's voice must be assumed to supply a natural transition from speech to song for any actress at all, no matter what the timbre of her speaking voice may be. If the other actress's singing is represented by Asha Bhonsle's voice, the improvement in verisimilitude is little, for the two sisters, as far as their voices are concerned, could be twins.

All this is part of the stylization of the film form in India, in which the song plays an inalienable part. Even if the gramophone and the record were available to the entire public

3

representing the film audience, it could not take the place of the film; for without the 'picturization' of the song, its enjoyment is not complete. Without the visual correlative of the music, in which an actor or actress may go through many fantastic and delectable motions, the song is a voice without a body, although the song, disembodied by the radio and the gramophone, is heard interminably. In many a house, the inmates would have to go without dinner if the cook did not have a transistor radio by his side. All-India Radio's commercial radio pours out film music throughout the average person's waking hours; yet the song is not autonomous by itself, it is a pleasurable reminder of the emotion of the scene, recollected in tranquility. The song, not only heard but 'seen' in its place at the climactic moment of drama and accompanied by inventive visual movements, many of them substituting for the climax to the sexual foreplay of the preceding scene, has become a 'must' to the popular audience. As soon as the preliminaries of love making lead up to the inevitable kiss and the sexual congress disallowed by the censor, the song provides a release from the tension into a kind of musical ejaculation. Attempts at the making of dramatically powerful films without songs have been at best lukewarmly received (*Kanoon, Achanak* and others) and in most cases, proved complete flops. Whether with the sophistication of the dramatic film and the growth of the public's opportunity to hear music outside the cinema theatre will ever lead to a separation of the two forms is difficult to say. At this point of time, it seems hardly likely.

As far as background music is concerned, most of our filmmakers are content to wield the baton over bowdlerized folk music with an Indian instrument thrown in now and then in order to fill up the vacuum of awkward silence. One of the early attempts to break out of the rut was, significantly, through a 'musical'. In *Kalpana,* Uday Shankar suddenly brought pure Indian music to the screen. Although not all background music, it showed how Indian music could find creative expression in the cinema. The first film to show the creative possibilities of Indian music in the cinema was, significantly again, in a film made by a foreigner. Jean Renoir's *The River* made some startling use of Indian music in the background. The sequence of kite-flying, for instance, was supported by Carnatic vocal *taans* which perfectly sketched the jerky yet rhythmical movements of the kite in the sky. The title music, traditionally a piece that requires a lot of 'body', consisted solely of a sitar and a pair of tablas. In its use of solo voices or instruments as pure background, it showed a dramatic grasp of Indian music which was superior to Vishnudas Shirali's predominantly 'dance' music for *Kalpana*. Shirali's later work on Films Division newsreels and documentaries show his failure to produce dramatically effective Indian background music. Ravi Shankar's attempts at producing orchestration with Indian instruments over the AIR met the fate which has overtaken all similar attempts by Timir Baran and others. What had succeeded as 'dance music' failed to become either 'pure music' or 'film music'. Perhaps the reason is that each major Indian instrument has a life of its own and is complete in itself. The sitar or the veena needs no other instrument, except for a percussion accompaniment, to complete its musical expression. In Western music, every note is conceived, as it were, in a co-existent relationship with other notes, and every instrument with others through orchestration. Harmony, counterpoint and tonal perspective express a certain dramatic conflict which reflects the realistic nature of Western thought, and these become even more useful in the 'descriptive music' that the cinema often requires. Indian music develops a melody through involutions within itself and in terms of a flowing line. It is by nature more contemplative than descriptive; it is more poetry than drama; more individual than social. A medley of instruments tends to dissipate the musical expression of the melody. The fewer the instruments, the truer the music has a chance to be. The notion that Indian music is, therefore, not 'dramatic' enough and does not have enough 'body' was hit hard by Renoir's *The River*. It showed that where the content is Indian—and it was particularly in certain sequences of *The River*—Indian music is perfectly suited to the film medium.

With *Pather Panchali* came the first film which was completely Indian and completely cinematic. Its music was, therefore, completely Indian too, for what would express the Indian mind and the Indian scene better than Indian music ?

The real problem arises in dealing with contemporary urban reality and this is now being faced by the younger film-makers in Bengal. In *Parash Pathar* Satyajit Ray produced a brilliant piece in the sequence of the taxi-ride after Paresh Babu has cashed in on his philosopher's stone for the first time. But the same success is not achieved in every sequence. Neither is it achieved in an otherwise notable film like Mrinal Sen's *Punashcha*, a story of love and frustration set in contemporary urban society. The plaintive notes of Indian melody seemed to suit the two-dimensional simplicity of the rural scene, but not the varied levels and the conflicting pressures of urban existence. A certain amount of instrumentation appears necessary here. The problem of Indian film music has thus at least arisen, and at least with some directors, it is no longer submerged in blissful ignorance.

It is interesting to examine the role of the so-called 'music-directors' in this context. Ravi Shankar, Ali Akbar Khan, Vilayet Khan, have all tried their hands at it. But it is only in association with an imaginative film director that they appear to have had any success. Ali Akbar Khan's music for Tapan Sinha's *Khsudita Pashan* is not half as inventive as his work in Ritwik Ghatak's *Ajaantrik*. It seems reasonable to conclude that worthy musicians as they are, their contribution to good film music is not as 'music directors' but rather as composers, the music director's function being carried out by the film director himself. It is the film director who, in the present situation, can give the lead in the creation of good film music.

The sixties, however, saw the emergence of a few who come closer to the concept of a film music director, in the area of background music. Vanraj Bhatia is surely the foremost on the strength of the work he did in some short films such as Shanti Chowdhury's *To Light a Candle*. A fully trained composer in Western music, he can integrate Indian and Western instruments in a meaningful way. However, his feeling for Indian music may not run as deep as for the Western to which he seems to be closer. Perhaps this contributes to his tendency to write the 'unheard' copybook film music rather than anything more venturesome. Vijay Raghav Rao has shown some imaginative ability (more forceful and assertive, but perhaps less sophisticated) in his work with Mrinal Sen, for instance, in *Bhuvan Shome*. His use of dissonance and concrete music elements within the Indian idiom, although a little overwrought at times, marks an interesting departure. It is a step, as Vanraj Bhatia's is, towards creating some programmatic equivalence with Indian urban, as opposed to rural, phenomena. The rhythm of rural life is still so seemingly regular and graceful despite grinding poverty that it is easier for Indian music with its solo bias and its folk tradition to fulfil its needs on the screen; it is urban life whose rhythm is too uncertain, too complex, too full of internal contradiction for the simple linear melody to reflect with sufficient conviction. This is not to say that emotional situations in rural scenes may not be complex or may not be simple in urban scenes; yet there seems to be a greater need for extra dimensions in the emerging industrial-urban realities of India.

What has been seen in the sixties by way of new music is not by itself a wide enough musical compass; nor does it take the music director beyond the somewhat uni-dimensional tendency, almost stereotyped, of heightening the given mood of the visual. Whether it is really possible for anyone other than the director of the film to use music counter to the mood in order to make a particular comment, is a difficult question to answer, and must depend on the extent to which a director with a personal vision is able to control the application of music just as he controls other inputs by his team into what in the end must be 'his' film. On the other hand, a film director who is capable of writing his own music is liable to have a more limited vocabulary than a professional's, even though his oneness with the film helps him to integrate the music with the other elements more closely than anyone else. An excellent instance of this is in *Charulata,* where Ray's own music, very spare in its outlines, has an immutability in its integration with the rest. As with *Pather Panchali's* folk-derived theme music (directed by Ravi Shanker), Ray succeeds in creating, with derivation from a composition of Rabindranath Tagore's, singularly apt for the film both in the words (not sung in the film) and in the tune, a *memorable* melody which becomes inextricably associated with the film. The use of the main theme, its variations and above all the timing and application of it is much subtler than in *Pather Panchali* whose theme relies much more directly on the appeal of the words (sung in the film by the old woman in her broken voice) and the melody of a well-known evocative-nostalgic folk song.

But the problem of film music is not an isolated problem at all. Background music is only one of the elements that goes into today's film-making and the line in which it develops must depend on the approach to the film as a whole. Its basic function is to give the film director another means of surmounting the limitation which the camera imposed upon him. Basically, the camera records faithfully what it sees before itself. It cannot indulge in purely 'subjective' expression as in literature. It cannot produce artistic distortion (except to an extremely limited extent) as the painter's brush or the sculptor's chisel. Music thus gives the film director a means of imparting a certain 'colour' to the image. It gives him equipment for both 'expressionist' and 'impressionist' use. In other words he can employ it either for purely subjective expression or for intensifying an objective impression given by the visual, sometimes referred to as 'unheard music'. He can associate a particular melody with a particular place, person or situation so as to be able to evoke its memory. Music can also be used as a comment, even a counterpoint running against the mood of the sequence. The tendency in the commercial cinema is always to use it to heighten the mood. Many significant directors use less and less of music in their work, replacing it by carefully selected effect sounds, or use music the way visuals are used, as part of the scene itself. Ritwik Ghatak in *Meghe Dhaka Tara* makes music part of the story itself, without in any way turning it into a musical; Antonioni in *La notte's* restaurant sequence gives it the value of effect sound, yet makes it profoundly meaningful; Satyajit Ray uses much less music (composed by himself) in *Charulata* in 1966 than he had done with Ravi Shankar's in *Pather Panchali* in 1955. Altogether music becomes a means of adding to the evocative power of the image and makes for a wider range of subjective expression.

The ability of Indian music to fulfil all these requirements in all types of films depends as much on the basis 'Indian-ness' of the directors' approach and attitudes, as on the further evolution of Indian music itself. Both classical and folk forms of Indian music were evolved for a society which has already changed a very great deal and is now in the throes of ever more rapid change. It would be foolish to be deluded by the fact that it continues to delight our ears and that we feel perfectly attuned to it. We enjoy it more as an evocation of the past; it gives us a deep subterranean sense of belonging to tradition. But tradition must move forward, and constantly develop into the present and evolve towards the future—in a continuous line in which there should, ideally, be no break. Indian music today is very largely an evocation of the past. It is not a living force born out of living society. Because the modern Indian feels the lack of a true link with tradition and is getting more and more drawn into unrelated Western forms superimposed on his life, he rediscovers and cherishes his sense of belonging to his own history in a communion with it through music. But this is a problem that is not special to films. The problem of being completely Indian and completely contemporary in thought and feeling is echoing through the entire range of Indian art.

1966

ᔓ the futility of
film censorship

I

Film censorship in any country is a difficult enough business, but nowhere is it as complicated as in India. For years, it has been under fire from the film industry for its 'double standard' in judging foreign and Indian films, from traditional-conservative circles for being too lax, from intellectual-progressive circles for being too restrictive, particularly in matters of sex and politics.

No matter how much fundamental unity we may have, our vast and ancient country, made up of a bewildering variety of religious, ethnic and linguistic groups with their different traditions, customs and habits, does not naturally develop uniform standards of countrywide applicability, especially when it is in the throes of change. Until the other day, a Bengali woman would have shuddered at the thought of going out with a flower in her hair, a Maharashtrian or South Indian woman would have been equally sad at the thought of going without it. For a woman to expose her navel would be considered shocking in the villages or small towns of the Punjab, but in neighbouring Rajasthan even the bared lower half of the breasts raises no eyebrows, while the exposed face causes shock. Travelling at dawn in Western Rajasthan, I once saw a row of colourfully clad women squatting along the riverside, performing their morning functions in full view of the main road. When I expressed mild surprise at the boldness of the proceedings, my Rajasthani companion explained that since the faces could not be identified (being fully covered), there was no cause for shame in the exposure of the bottoms.

In such a country, only the middle class with its English education in common can venture to lay down rules for the nation's reactions to nudity, partial or complete. But even this middle class is too divided to agree on the measurement of exposure deemed ethical for the Indian eye. Some quote the *Kamasutra,* Kalidas and Konarak; others condemn any acknowledgement of the existence of sex in the name of Indian tradition and culture (of which their ignorance must be profound). It has been pointed out that the puritanical souls of today have obtained their inspiration not from Indian culture but from foreign missionaries for whose teachings their minds had already been prepared by the puritanism of Aurangzeb. Witness the effect of missionary teaching on the aboriginals regarding their clothes, destroying their sense of colour and design and unity with environment, imposing the vulgarity of the pink bra, introducing the idea of sin where none existed.

But this un-Indian puritanical streak spread beyond the proselytized into a large section of the middle class, not excluding the leadership of the country. Not only Gandhiji but, to a lesser extent, Tagore and Nehru came under the influence and accepted it as a part of their synthesis of East and West. Tagore's poetry in the early and middle periods has traditionally sensuous turns of phrase and guiltless moments of ecstasy over female lips and breasts; his novels and his prose generally are much more restrained and in his later poetry he would not dream of using much of his earlier stock in trade in matters of sex.

As the nineteenth-century Bengal Renaissance progressed into the twentieth, it became more and more puritanical. Its leaders had been brought up on Victorian and pre-World War I English social and literary ideals and stuck to them even after England shook them off with the changing times. In true colonial style, India became the last outpost of British Victorian morality and remains so in the period of Independence. Victorian hypocrisies are today an integral part of the middle-class mind. It is not the British censor who stopped kissing on the Indian screen. They were only concerned with political censorship, and brought in the kiss barrier, against which the film industry protests endlessly today, only in response to the outcries of self-appointed guardians of public morality. The vigour of some of the kisses of the Indian prewar screen would put contemporary Hollywood films to shame.

A Films Division documentary made up of interviews with people on the subject of family planning ran into trouble because village women described sex too frankly for the genteel city folk sitting in judgement on them in censor panels. Yet one of the problems which has dogged family planning work is the lack of frankness. There is a famous true story to illustrate this : a man used condoms but made his wife pregnant; he had put one on his thumb, 'exactly as the doctor had shown him'. The millions who march through the Puri Jagannath temple every Rathajatra day are hardly bothered about some of the world's boldest erotic display on the walls before them. Yet the procreation chapter of the *Vrihadaran-yakopanishad* is left untranslated by most modern pundits. The middle-class woman's dress has hurriedly changed from its traditional modes of exposure towards more covering (the exceptions are the very fashionable few). The middle class itself is the quickest to close its eyes and ears when confronted with the wealth of Indian erotic art and literature.

But too much is made of sex whenever censorship is discussed. The censorship of political and social portrayals is much more severe and has far more serious consequences compared to which the problems with sex are of little importance. The cinema is virtually the only medium which establishes some communication with the illiterate masses and can most vividly hold up social and political problems to the people in general; yet social and political controversy in the cinema is virtually impossible. The slight, and brief, freedom given to some late sixties' documentaries (*India 1967, Face to Face*) is nothing compared to the shackles of the feature film.

The cinema cannot be used as a means of national debate; it must conform to the ideas of the Establishment. The Prime Minister can be criticised in the press but not in the cinema. Show a doctor neglecting patients in a hospital if you dare.

People are kept waiting and everybody demands bribes in a government office—impossible! The 'Gandhi cap' was objected to in Satyajit Ray's *Parash Pather* because the wearer of such a cap must automatically have a milk-white soul. Ray shrewdly pointed out that Gandhiji never wore such a cap and saved the day. Similarly even his very sympathetic portrayal of an Anglo-Indian girl in *Mahanagar* created a minor furore in Parliament. The miracle sequence in Fellini's *La dolce vita* was taken out because it might offend the susceptibilities of the Indian Christian minority (while it is shown extensively in Christian countries, including the Pope's own, where it was made in the first place).

No member of any political party, any profession, can be shown as corrupt, except for the village moneylender who cannot put up a defence. We live in the best of all possible worlds; there are some minor troubles, like the burning of Harijans, but the government is attending to them and everything will be all right very soon.

Many people pass sweeping judgements on foreign films on the score of their frankness about sex while defending this benign view of Indian society. The intellectual ferment of the West seeks answers to the problems of affluence and good films have played a big part in making people think, in attacking established ideas, in exposing the hypocrisy of the mealy-mouthed. Religion, ethics, politics, customs, traditions—nothing has been spared from the questioning, sometimes attack, in the films of many famous directors.

If hypocrisies could be put aside and Indian reality portrayed frankly on the Indian screen, not only would we have delectable views of the navels of Rajasthan and the breasts of Bastar State, the lean midriffs of Andhra, the bare shoulders of Manipur, the leg contours of Maharashtra, and the bare backs of Gujarat; we would see a fearfully revealing scene of greed, violence, pettiness, indifference to suffering, cynicism, casteism, nepotism, falsehood, cruelty, the world's most massive prostitution, bribery, jobbery and corruption—all of which the censorship seeks to hide behind the sanctimonious hypocrisy which is the hallmark of this country's middle-class morals and a large part of its political and social leadership.

It is possible to go on ad infinitum criticising censorship in this vein, but to no purpose. The film industry's own attitudes must be examined first. Take the so-called double standard, the cross of which the film industry has been bearing so long. Out of nearly 6,000 cinema theatres in the country, about 40 regularly show foreign language films (at the time of writing). It is hard to see how the impact of a different set of standards in these can affect attendance at Indian films more than marginally. Besides, if sex and violence predominate in the films imported, then something should be done about the import policy first, because a great many good films without these ingredients from all over the world never get shown in Indian theatres at all. Coordination between the ministries of Information & Broadcasting and Commerce on this point has been overdue for some time; as a result, India has failed to keep her international promise of importing at least thirty films from outside the USA and Britain which she made in order to hold the 1965 film festival. Finally, the censors' view that foreign films represent a different way of life is perfectly valid, and to impose Indian social standards on them in toto would be patently absurd.

The belly-aching of the film industry over its censorship troubles is largely hypocritical. If liberal political censorship were introduced, would the commercial cinema rush into the making of adult, intelligent, thought-provoking films like *Judgement at Nuremberg* without making the judges sing around a tree, or *Advise and Consent* without senators dancing, *The Best Man* without making the election of the Prime Minister look like a nightclub sequence ? Would the relaxation of taboos on sex result in witty, humane films like Milos Forman's *Love and the Blonde;* if rape scenes are allowed to be more frank, will they result in films of the stark poetry of Ingmar Bergman's *Virgin Spring ?* The fact is that with very minor exceptions, the commercial cinema will not pursue any real controversies, and in matters of sex, would prefer suggestiveness to frankness. Nudity by itself, once its novelty wears off, is not titillating, nightclubs all over the world have experience of this and so have film industries. Nudity in the commercial cinema will be closer to striptease than to the Didargunj *Yakshi*.

The all-India film has been a reactionary, conformist force ever since the early years of World War II; it no longer crusades against casteism or the dowry system or advocates Hindu-Muslim amity. Its formula is to juxtapose extremes of tradition (virtue) and Westernization (sin), to prevent the synthesis of East and West, tradition and modernity, which Tagore and Nehru set as the ideals of the country, and to return to its comfortable notions of Rama and Sita after giving it the vicarious satisfactions of sin without contaminating itself. In the end, tradition must triumph, no matter how superstitious it may be. With increased freedom in matters of sex, the commercial cinema will become still more suggestive than frank; with political taboos removed, it will make a travesty of politics by turning it into a song and dance routine.

Liberalized censorship can benefit the film only on the plane of art; it can make the average commercial film worse than today. I am not making an artificial distinction between art and commerce; we know that the two can occasionally meet and that art cannot exist in the total absence of commerce. It is only a hypothetical distinction made for convenience.

III

Two basic questions arise from any discussion of film censorship in India. Firstly, whose standards, in a multi-levelled society, are to be applied as uniform standards ? Secondly, is it possible to apply a uniform standard between art and non-art ?

We know that censorship will never please everybody. Then whom should it please ? What national norms, if any, should it serve? Obviously, the best compromise (and nothing but a compromise is in practice possible in such matters) is to make it consistent with the total idea of society embodied in the Constitution and implied in the statements and attitudes of those national leaders on whose ideas the country's major institutions and goals are based.

The basic cultural component of the vision of development in India proceeds from a synthesis of East and West, tradition and modernity. For more than a hundred years, progress in India has been brought about from this premise : India will retain her tradition and identity but keep modifying them dynamically with the progress of science, technology and the new philosophies arising from them. The cultural definition of this idea received its widest and greatest embodiment in Tagore ; politically and economically it was developed as the main plank of the Nehru vision of India, on which the countries' major policies are still based. Many of Gandhiji's ideas, revered as they are in themselves, no longer form the basic tenets of the country. His views on family planning, industrialization, and non-violence, for instance, have either fallen by the wayside or been modified beyond recognition. Mahatmaji's ideas on sex, let us face it, will not do. He was in favour of defacing the erotic sculptures of Konarak and Khajuraho; the proposal shocked Tagore, and Nehru had a good road to Konarak built. Of course it is impossible to use Tagore or Nehru as a textbook from which to compile censorship rules; but at least the direction can be seen in the extent to which Tagore and writers holding similar moral attitudes admitted the existence of sex or presented nudity in their literature or Nehru allowed the voice of the opposition to be heard and be taken as a point of reference in framing the concept of the rules.

Nor will the suppression of debate of any kind ease the dilemma. Tagore and many others of his persuasion, who despite their advocacy of the Satyam-Shivam-Sundaram tenet, strongly attacked superstition, corruption and other evils, were traditional enough to write passionate descriptive poems of physical love and novels of great depth in love experience. They did shrink from the violent, gory, details of love-making or violence and minute descriptions of total ugliness in character. These limits, set by people who believed in persuasion more than in force, may not go far enough for the extremist; but they will in practice represent an enormous liberation over the standards applied today. They will at least be consistent with the officially set goals, attitudes and principles of our

present society for its self-attainment. It will prevent puritanical, obscurantist, oppressive sections of society from dominating censorship. It follows that people should be nominated
to censor panels not for the sake of representing this or that
sector of society but for representing the trends of thought
underlying the country's goals. This will result in greater
homogeneity in the panels and prevent wildly different deci-
sions. At present, the fate of a film often depends on the
question : Which four members of the panel are coming to
see it ?

IV

Most of the arguments against strict censorship are made from
the point of view of art; most of the actual use of liberal
censorship is made from the point of non-art. The attempt
to apply the same standards to all films irrespective of their
integrity, moral and artistic value has turned film censorship
in India into a farce of measurements. Whether it is overtly
admitted or not, some element of quality judgement is inevitable in intelligent censorship. Unless the principle is admitted that the need and the justification of frankness in a film
is in the honesty and integrity of a film and not on the boundaries of what is physically shown, it is useless even to discuss
the reform of censorship. Liberalization without this understanding would only mean a greater amount of 'exploitation'
and sensationalism in commercial cinema; stringent regulation
will prevent the honest artistic film of controversy or love from
being made. The whole idea of applying what, for lack of
a more comprehensive phrase, I have indicated as 'Tagore-
Nehru' standard, is dependent on a sharp differentiation between art and non-art in intent and performance. There will
be dispute, inevitably, on who is and who is not entitled to
pronounce one work to be art and deny that status to another.
But this is a difficulty in all forms of choice, and must be faced.

There may be some truth in the contention that whatever is
permissible in literature and the other arts is not automatically
permissible in the cinema because everything is too concretely
present on the cinema screen which is seen by a multitude

sitting together.   However, far too much is made of this contention and all freedom is squeezed out under its doubtful
sanction.   The gap between what is permitted in the other
arts and the cinema as art must be narrowed down.

Having said all this, it is necessary to add for the sake of
realism that the censor can seldom be more liberal than the
public whom he serves.   If there is a glorification of hypocrisy in our society, then it will inevitably find some reflection
not only in our films, but in our censorship as well.   But when
was society reformed without defying some sections of it?

Barua :
legend and reality

Rarely has a film-maker been as much of a legendary hero as Pramathesh Barua (1903-1951), prince of Gauripur, Assam, aristocrat, horseman, marksman, dancer, tennis player, hunter, music lover, 'foreign-travelled' actor and director—his image was of an irresistible Prince Charming descended among common folk, honouring them by his very presence in their midst. As director, he combined art with box office, revolt with conformity, sentiment with cynicism, virtue with vice; what more could one want ? No other actor had created a type with such enduring influence on the mainstream of the Indian film —an influence which spread beyond Bengal into Hindi cinema and persists to this day. No personality in the cinema had established more identity between his private life and the films he created, the roles he played. His films were not objective records or interpretations of the work of others; they were intensely personal. He did not merely make *Debdas*. He *was* 'Debdas'.

This one character typified so much of him, and exercised such fascination over later film-makers and audiences, that its roots are worth searching for. Saratchandra Chatterjee wrote *Debdas* at the age of seventeen. It is the story of a young man born of a wealthy family of the landed aristocracy who falls in love with Parvati, a playmate of his childhood, daughter of a poor neighbour. When Debdas goes off to Calcutta for higher studies, Parvati, yielding to her father's wishes like a good Hindu daughter, marries the man of his choice, although she continues to love Debdas. Debdas comes to know of the marriage, takes to drink and to a

4

prostitute who promptly falls for him and gets ready to
leave her profession for him. Parvati, hearing of this, comes
to see him but fails to deflect him from his downward path.
Debdas wastes away in spite of all the care lavished on him
by Chandra, the prostitute. When he is desperately ill, he
keeps his promise to Parvati to come to her when the time was
ripe and dies at her doorstep. The body is burnt at a pyre
while inside the house Parvati eats her heart out at the fate
of the man she loves.

No wonder the story endeared itself to the public. Rich
young man pines away for village belle, powerless against
society, wallowing in delicious self-pity; his indulgence in
drink calls forth sympathy instead of condemnation because
it is due to unrequited love; even the prostitute showers
upon him a sort of comforting mother-love, touched by his
suffering and drawn by his good looks; the passage of years
does nothing to dim the light of Parvati's eternal love for
him. Which man would not like to be loved so and which
woman resist mothering such handsome waywardness? Saratchandra repeated many of the characters of this novel in
others that he wrote—the weak hero languishing for lack of
love denied him by society, the fallen woman, more full of
virtue than her chaste compatriots, who mothers the hero,
delinquent genius, dying poet. The *Srikanta* series, *Charitrahin*,
are all variations of these types and situations. His heroes
never make a positive protest against society; they turn to
drink, seek the benevolent nursing of a woman or a series
of women — and find it so readily that they must have
some secret understanding with the feminine race. Tagore
fashioned and embodied the 'Young Bengal' hero with his
vigorous urge to build a new society free of superstition;
Saratchandra spoke for those who failed at (or were too
weak even to give) battle and sought refuge in mother-love.
The love for which they supposedly languish is basically self-
love; there is nothing outgoing in it, no sense of concern
about humanity, no urge to change the world to one's own
vision. Saratchandra outgrew this self-love in some of his
mature work, particularly his long stories like *Pallisamaj*,
Pandit Mashai or works like *Bindur Chheley, Mejdidi, Ramer*

Sumati, where his descriptive power engages itself fully and leaves his own autobiographical biases aside. Barua wedded himself to the seventeen-year-old author of *Debdas,* and never outgrew its adolescent syndrome.

The basic difference between Saratchandra and Tagore reflected itself in the work of Barua, except that his cinematic ability never matched Saratchandra's literacy prowess. The difference lay in Tagore's ability to identify the forces of change in our impact with Western civilization and his dynamic synthesis of these with our own tradition. Saratchandra's vision was not of such sweep; its main concerns were more insular, less able to relate themselves clearly to the forces that changed the face of India and continue to do so.

The historical importance of both Saratchandra and Barua lies in the fact that the male sex symbol they built up as weak hero in need of feminine domination was not just a creature of their fancy, but embodied a familiar type in real life, particularly in Bengal. It is the adolescent incapable of action to realise his own ambition, seeking solution in escape, who drowns himself in a lake of unrequited love after writing a lot of puerile verse; the adolescent who has not yet become a man — and will never be.

But even in the outpourings of adolescence there is a social protest; *Debdas* points to the inhumanity of arranged marriages forced on the lovers due to their social differences, although Barua does not develop this theme, being too obsessed with the romantic hero, that is, himself. In *Mukti,* the opposite theme is brought out — the theme of the separation of a couple unable to love each other. Again it is a theme of social reform, years ahead of its time; but Barua leaves this starting point to go into a fantastic pastoralia. The romantic young painter, anxious to liberate his wife for another marriage, pretends to commit suicide, actually disappearing into the jungles of Assam. There they meet again with the new husband in attendance, and he rescues her from kidnappers, himself getting killed in the process. Once more the adolescent has bought bravado in self-immolation to spite society.

If the secret of Barua's popularity lay in the easy appeal

of this sociological content, his legendary fame among Indian, particularly Bengali film-makers, was in his creative fervour and his technical inventiveness. There is no doubt that his films were the products of the creative passion of one man and not of a team of technicians who had nothing of their own to say, an experience far too common in Bengal these days. He wrote his own scripts, acted and directed his films, exercised firm control over all departments of film-making. Vague and immature as it was, there was some sort of philosophy and passion in his films which reflected the artistic predilections of the less advanced middle class of his time (the literature of this period is far more sophisticated). To dialogue he brought a degree of naturalness unknown to Bengali cinema of his time, although today it may sound stilted. 'This is not dialogue, this is the way to talk' is a reaction quoted by Barnouw and Krishnaswamy in their book *Indian Film*. His integrity towards his own notions of art is evident in the way he spurned lucrative offers from Bombay. 'It is not my field,' he said, 'it is a bazaar'.

In his own acting there was an impassive underplaying which, in contrast to the melodrama of his themes, produced an effect of heroism. Others turned in memorable performances for him — Chandrabati in *Debdas* for instance, as the prostitute who loves the hero (the milieu of prostitution is subtly created). Yet one cannot jump to any conclusions regarding his directing ability, for there are some very bad examples of acting in his films — Jamuna's own for example. There are passages in *Debdas* in which Jamuna goes 'off' as soon as she stops speaking, exactly as on the stage where expressions are less visible and attention shifts more markedly to the next speaker.

Some of his cutting was meaningful and made for dramatic brevity, as in the way he established the relationship of Debdas and Parvati in a montage of three or four shots or reflected Debdas's agony in the furious sounds of the train. The reflection of Chandra in a fraction of a mirror after she has come back to her haunt and is asking after Debdas, the shot of her in the carriage listening to Debdas's song or of her sitting desolately at the window in contrast to the noisy vulgarity of her clients inside — these and many other such fragments testify to an intermittent groping towards the particular values of the cinema. But they lie side by side with many immature, heavy and strident attempts at symbolism — the opening doors of *Mukti* (if Hitchcock had not achieved anything else in *Spellbound,* he would have been damned for ever for that one shot), or the infamous 'telepathic shots' in *Debdas,* the dwindling candle to suggest impending death. There are some intelligent uses of the close-up, the flash-back; but there are equally unintelligent outbursts of song so reminiscent of the *jatra* or folk theatre. There are again some interesting uses of detail. On the other hand, the films appear sketchy in their treatment and development of the theme, lacking sadly in that mundane detail which makes up the fabric of reality and full of contradictory sociological and technical elements. He borrowed from the West (he made frequent trips abroad and was for some time an observer at Elstree) and from the folk theatre, drawing inspiration from social protest and social conformity (as in the conventional glorification of rural as against urban life). We find that his work shows relatively well-composed interiors and badly framed outdoor scenes, the rooms often composed in diagonals at a junction of the walls, but with the characters lined up horizontally and in a 'front-oriented' manner very like his horizontal, parallel lines deadening the landscape.'

What held back this jumble from any real artistic resolution was the appalling lack of taste. No painting deserved the slashing it got more than the ugly, ugly nude of *Mukti* which is supposed to testify to the artist's need for freedom. A lesser awareness of the values of painting is hardly conceivable and makes the claims made on behalf of art ludicrous. The decor in practically all his films, particularly when showing affluence, is full of the worst possible taste. His genius was a little too untutored, his level of appreciation of the other arts too low. As a result, his romanticism ran away with itself; nothing falls into place because nothing is solidly founded on terra firma, all his notions float indeterminately in some non-existent space. Realism, symbolism and fancy remain unsynthesized, and an excessive projection of self overwhelms the illusion of reality which narrative cinema demands.

It is necessary to spell out these aspects because of the unreal adulation of Barua which still pervades the older generation of film-makers in Bengal. Many of them who remember Barua with rapture have only to see his films today to realise how much they have dated, unlike many European — and Indian — films of earlier or contemporary periods. By 1935, when *Debdas* made its appearance, some of the world's greatest films — those of Chaplin, Eisenstein, Karl Dreyer, Pabst — had been made. To see Dreyer's *The Passion of Joan of Arc* (1928) today is still an intense spiritual experience; the film has not dated in the least, it could have been made yesterday. World cinema has hardly surpassed the excellence of some of the films made before and during the period of Barua in Bengal — a fact we tend to miss in the insularity of our vision. Jagirdar's *Ramshastri* and *Sant Tukaram* are in content and treatment much more mature achievements; Debaki Bose's films reflect much more of Bengal; Modhu Bose's show a more honest, primitive vigour, greater humour, and consistency.

Yet Barua's influence has been greater than of these others (especially in the average Bengali cinema, an undying one) because of the easy fascination exercised by his image of the doomed hero with his worn looks and ruffled hair, perpetually pampered by women. But more than this perhaps it was the uniqueness of his personal vision, whose quality may be debatable but whose intensity is beyond doubt. His shades are visible even in Guru Dutt's *Pyaasa* and *Kaghaz ka Phool* and in many others in Bombay's more virile if less idealistic dream factory. It is only sometime after he has been debunked that a proper appraisal of Barua can be made; without it, his historical and relative value tends either to be inflated beyond all proportions, or forgotten altogether.

1967

✑ Satyajit Ray :
the first ten years

I

Pather Panchali has been called the first *Indian* film. It is contemporary in the sense in which Amrita Sher-Gil's painting of South Indian priests is contemporary. It is India as seen by a contemporary artist who has found a point of contact not only with the present but also with the past and the future.

Why does it show such abject poverty ? Because that is the reality that thinking Indians must face. They must not only face it, but identify themselves with it in some way. To Bengalis whose lives were based for a hundred years on the nineteenth-century maxim, 'Speak in English, think in English, dream in English', such identification is not an easy process. It is a process of the discovery of India, of seeking one's roots in one's own soil, through which thinking men must pass not only in Bengal but in the whole country. From Rammohan Roy to Mahatma Gandhi, Rabindranath Tagore to Nehru, it is a history of the discovery of India which has come as a result of the discovery of the West.

With Independence, this process has been accelerated and has widened, particularly among artists and intellectuals. There is a certain nostalgia, a sense of homecoming, in this discovery of one's own country. The tremendous gulf that has separated the educated and the uneducated, the haves and the have-nots for generations intensifies this nostalgia and the deep desire for a spiritual identification with one's own people.

In Rabindranath Tagore's *Gora*, the hero of the novel is, unknown to himself, of foreign extraction. Yet he constantly opposes superficial criticism and reform of the beliefs of the people; for, first of all, he wants to be one of them, to understand them, and accept them. It is only from the point of identification, says Gora, that change becomes possible. India is on the threshold of such change, and identification is the essential precondition for it.

And *Pather Panchali* sees not only the poverty, but also the hope. It sees the beautiful in the midst of the ugly, love in the midst of meanness born of want. It does not draw a sentimental-romantic picture of *Sonar Bangla* of traditional Bengali literature. The images of the stooping old unwanted woman, whose hair is like a Medusa's and whose skin has more wrinkles than the oldest banyan tree in India, make the shining faces of the children stand out as images of life and hope as against death, despair, and cruelty. When Harihar wipes his armpit with the end of his dhoti, or extracts fish-bones from an uneven row of discoloured teeth, the images are of such complete ugliness that they make you shudder. But they are what make the children's first sight of a railway train, leaving a trail of smoke over the white field of *kash* flowers, so intensely beautiful.

Let us look at the story of the Apu trilogy. A little brahmin boy is born in one of the 5,58,000 villages of India; he has a sister and an old aunt, his intellectually-minded father, and his jealous, ever-watchful mother. His sister dies; the family leaves the village, goes to Banaras, the oldest of India's cities. Time comes for the father to pass away, amidst a flutter of pigeons. The boy is absorbed in himself and in the impressions of the world around him. For a while they have to go back to village life. He goes to a village school and, through his teacher, has a vision of the wider world. His lonely mother wants to keep her son under her wings, but he chafes under the restraint. He goes to the big city; he studies in a college. He reaches out to an even wider world which beckons to him and takes him further and further away from his mother.

On an evening when the stars are reflected in the water

and the fire flies dance, his mother dies. Life still goes on and, in fact, there is a sense of release from all bondage, mingled with grief. He is a young man now, and he falls in love with the girl whom he has married by accident. And then she dies, too, after a brief period of deep understanding and love. He feels he has lost everything; he blames his child for having caused the death of its mother. He wanders around without purpose, turning almost into a hermit. But forces of life assert themselves again; he reconciles himself to his fate, seeks out his son and, once more, finds a meaning in life.

This is the story of the trilogy. All the three films are not of uniform quality throughout but, taken together, they convey a sense of resignation, of infinite patience and yet also of hope.

There is no doubt that, as with so many others in Bengal, Ray's starting point is Tagore. Look at the heroes. Soumitra Chatterjee's resemblance to the young Tagore in *Apur Sansar* is far from accidental, for he reappears, without the beard, in film after film. The urge to break out of the confines of a traditional India fragmented into villages complete in themselves is planted in Apu's young mind in *Aparajito*. Bibhuti Bhushan Bandyopadhay's Apu, too, had more than a touch of innocence, wonder and the urge to explore; he was an idealist, but so much of a seer of visions that in later novels such as *Debajan* he becomes an angel. Tagore's protagonists are also without cynicism, but are more firmly rooted in social realities, and, like Gora, find themselves disillusioned by the pressure of hard facts. Ray's trilogy veers away from Bibhuti Bhushan's slightly dewy-eyed vision of 'Sonar Bangla' to a Tagorean outlook of someone who is deeply Indian and emerges from the heart of tradition but reaches out towards Western science with the urge to create a new Indian identity. At the end of *Aparajito* (the book), its hero sails forth to unknown seas leaving his son behind. Ray's Apu stays on terra firma, finds a new reason for living in his son. Bibhuti Bhusan's wonder child never grows up; Ray's Apu lives through the experiences of childhood, adolescence and youth to become a man.

In *Debi*, we meet Soumitra Chatterjee again, by now already an embodiment of Bengali youth of a certain period and type, both of which are distinctly derived from Tagore. The headmaster of *Aparajito* has now become the Brahmo professor, and continues to develop his teaching on lines already laid down : reach out to the outside world, conquer superstition, absorb the best of the West and apply it to your life to achieve a new synthesis. Already in *Debi,* the weakness of the character has also become apparent; he is a thinker more than a man of action, a bit of a Hamlet. He has read Mill and Bentham and disapproves of his father's superstitious visions, but he is not strong enough to withstand the pressures of tradition or to repudiate what he considers to be the evils of ignorance. In his political thinking, Tagore eschewed both the violence of the terrorist and the shrewdly practical non-violence of Gandhiji; but he provided great inspiration towards the general ideals of a patriotism which is not narrow, an individualism which is not intolerant. Ray's heroes also represent a noble philosophical outlook but are not men of action on the plane of grim reality.

In *Samapti,* Soumitra Chatterjee as Amulya carries a portrait of Napoleon with him wherever he goes (I am not suggesting that Tagore's philosophy had Gaullist undertones; the significance is in the ever-present image of the Western world, although outwardly the action is meant to indicate a period). He does assert himself in the marriage of his choice (unlike Apu of *Apur Sansar* who falls in love after an accidental marriage), but we know that he would not have pressed the point had his mother been as strong a character as the father in *Debi*. In *Charulata,* Soumitra has evolved further from his early Tagorean base; the Mill-Bentham-reading, Rammohan Roy-inspired character now belongs to the older generation and is embodied in the bearded, pince-nez-sporting Bhupati with his affluent idealism. Amal himself stands in between the pure Tagore and what is to come after. But he, too, is devoid of cynicism, on the whole un-self-conscious, and is capable of noble action, as in going away when he realises that he was about to betray his brother as much as the absconding misappropriator in whom his brother had placed so much trust. Of what is to come after we see rather more in *Kapurush;* the 'Rabindrik' generation has finally revealed its failure in the weak-minded, slightly parasitic intellectual (a film story-writer) who is made a coward not by his conscience but by sheer lack of courage.

In the series of films — the trilogy, *Debi, Samapti, Charulata* and *Kapurush,* the Ray hero has emerged in a straight line from the purely Tagorean mould of protected innocence into the contemporary world only to find himself inadequate to contend with the forces. The fact that Amitabha fails to take away Karuna with him on their second meeting may be outwardly a congenital weakness of character, but it also reveals that in his evolution, the type of hero represented by Soumitra Chatterjee in various Ray films is no longer noble in his motives and irresolute in his actions; he is now weak without being noble. But it is an end which is surely not untypical of the Bengali youth brought up under the Tagore umbrella. They have become cynical under the pressures of reality in independent India; but their past idealism has become a drag on them and has made them unable to cope with a society where, whether we like it or not, the law of the jungle has acquired some currency. But even this evolution never takes the hero entirely outside the Tagore value-world; it only takes him to its furthest limits, limits which Tagore himself had explored.

Even through the working-class garb of *Abhijan,* the Tagore-oriented middle-class minds of Ray and Chatterjee show clearly through the thin disguise of the different-style beard of its hero. Soumitra has tried in many ways to play 'tough' not only in this film but in others; but he has not ceased to represent the charm, innocence, un-self-consciousness and the accompanying weakness of the young Bengali romantic hero of the Tagore and immediate post-Tagore periods. A sort of protected hero, with a dominating father-figure lurking somewhere in the shadows, imbued with a touching faith in ultimate justice, who is not destined to battle on his own, still less to win.

Let us examine the other protagonists of Ray's films. *Jalsaghar* does not bring out the rising generation at all;

it is concerned with the passing one, and represents the fore-
going in reverse, as it were. With his very Indian predilection
for avoiding conflict and drama, Ray subdues the new capitalist
of the original story to a buffoon and lavishes his sympathy
on the decadent landlord. Because of his and our certain
knowledge of his impermanence, this is not a backward-
looking film at all; the sadness is only one of parting. But
what concerns us here is that the hero of *Jalsaghar* belongs
to the same era; it would have been altogether too obvious if he had had a forward-looking son, but this would
no doubt have projected the sociological framework represented
by his film.

The same Chhabi Biswas appears in *Kanchanjangha*; and
his relationship with the cheeky young chap who wants his
daughter but would turn down his offer of a job could have
been that of old-time father and modern son; or could it ?
Here the hero comes from an altogether new social class,
and the line of his thought seems different from that of the
Tagorean dreamers. He is a product of today, with an aggres-
sive idealism that is more capable of contending with realities,
because it is more clear-eyed and much more of a piece.
He is not the affluent son turned idealist; he belongs more to
the larger middle classes which ceased to be zemindars long
ago or had never been. He is not in the least ashamed of
his comical uncle, would call a spade a spade any day, and
even if he is attracted to the impossible Rai Bahadur's daughter,
he sets no great store by her vague promise of seeing him in
Calcutta; and if the liaison did not work out, he would have
no hesitation in breaking with it. But this different hero
is only hinted at in the splendid isolation of Darjeeling and
the lightweight film obliquely bypasses a set of values which
is unfamiliar to the Tagore mythology.

The sole connection one could see between this and *Parash
Pathar* is that the *Kanchanjangha* hero's uncle could have
found the touchstone and behaved exactly the same way as
Paresh Babu. The young secretary played by Kali Banerjee
is so healthy, so devoid of either the nobility or the cowardice
of the Soumitra-heroes that when he swallows the touchstone,
his powerful metabolism leads to the complete digestion of

it. But again, it is a character in the background seen at a distance, and without a great deal of signification.

Another modern type, much less of a hero, is presented by Anil Chatterjee in *Postmaster* and *Mahanagar*. But in both films, the basic emphasis is away from him; in one it is on the child, in the other, the woman. As a result he is a somewhat shadowy figure compared to the other heroes and is only brought in to fill a place for the traditional, none-too-bright middle-class individual. He has acquired the outward mental accoutrement of the Tagore world to the extent of wanting to teach the child in *Postmaster* and counselling his wife to take a job in *Mahanagar*, without any sense of dedication to either. His relationships, his emotions never reach the larger-than-life size that other Ray heroes, especially Soumitra Chatterjee, do in their representation of an epoch or in embodying an outlook.

II

One could say that in the films preceding *Mahanagar*, the preoccupation is with man. Wowen like Indira Thakrun, Sarbajaya and Aparna are important enough; but they do not supply the motive force of the films. They are the familiar women of Indian tradition, loving and sometimes loved, providers of anchorage to the nomadic male who goes out to do battle and whose fate therefore is of greater importance. The girl in *Debi* is not much more than an object owned by her father-in-law more than even by her husband; even Sarbajaya, patient and loving in a mother-earth way, cannot decide the future, either of her own or of her family. None of them have, or are aware of having, an existence of their in their own right. Paresh Babu's wife grows rich with him and poor again; she breaks into a magnificent smile of happiness when the gold turns into iron after the secretary has digested the touchstone, but she could not have brought about their renewed poverty, however much she might have wanted it. In *Jalsaghar* the wife is a non-entity, the other woman, an entertainer. In *Postmaster*, the child is a little mother already burdened with the responsibilities of an outgoing love; in *Samapti,* the scene of examining the bride brings out all the comicality of such arrangements, and although Mrinmoyee protests first, when she welcomes the bonds of marriage, she does so in a way not materially different from that of other brides. Although the husband is a somewhat 'enlightened' young man, the measure of self-determination which the wife is destined to have does not seem to be too great. It does record a change in the outlook towards marriage, but more from the man's point of view than from that of the girl who accepts with happiness what all others have accepted before her.

It is in *Mahanagar* that for the first time, we come across a woman who is awakened to the possibility of determining the course of her own life. Typically enough, the awakening touch comes from the husband, for men have been traditional liberators of women. But traditionally, too, they have retracted when they have found the consequences of their action, the undermining of their overlordship. Arati is unable to exert herself to retain her brief freedom, but she has had a glimpse of a world in which she is somebody in her own right, and when she hands in her resignation, it is not in obedience to her husband's wish, but to her own impulsive fellow feeling for the Anglo-Indian girl who is unjustly dismissed. It is her one act of protest against society, and she carries it out in a sphere where she means something in her own right. Ironically enough, in this act she also gives up the freedom she has won. Somebody, protesting against this thesis when I touched upon it in an article, said that 'as for her rights, Arati is perverted'. So she is; the adjustment to a sudden inner feeling of economic independence is not easy; it comes out in little awkward ways which add to the truth of the situation.

But I find Ray's first essay on the Indian woman tentative and unsure of itself. As a result, the characters are not seen sufficiently from the inside, and there is excessive — uncharacteristic for Ray — dependence on the outward incident. The meeting under the doorway where the husband says, 'Do not worry, it is a vast city, and one of us is bound to find a job' — provides too pat a solution for a problem which will

continue to plague us for a long time to come. It is unlike
Ray to seek such four-square solutions; his films are much
better when they are what some people these days call 'open
ended'. Consider his lack of partisanship in *Debi*, his
sympathy for the decaying zemindar in *Jalsaghar*.

The sureness of touch is much more evident in *Charulata*
and because Ray's understanding of her is perfect, everything
falls into place and ceases to look contrived. The character
is observed entirely from the inside — objectively so, in fact,
with the result that we do not see the interior of the minds
of the men. Except when he breaks down in the carriage
after the terrible discovery, Bhupati is more of a type than
a character — very agreeable, representative of the 'Young
Bengal' liberal, affluent Indian seeking-synthesis-with-Western
science, touching in his idealism, innocence and lack of self-
consciousness. Amal, too, reveals himself only in the scene
after the robbery, in the press room, when, standing there in
the half light behind his brother kneeling before the printing
machine, he awakens to the truth of his situation — that he,
too, like the robbing relative, was about to betray him. In
another scene when, in the midst of singing, he playfully
holds his sister-in-law in a near-embrace, he shows embarrass-
ment necessary to the situation. Yet, even in this scene, he
fulfils a requirement rather than revealing himself as he does
in the press room scene. His inner conflict is so muted as
to be missed by the correspondent mentioned earlier in her
protest against my interpretation.

But where Charulata herself is concerned, Ray achieves
that wonderful transparency in the objective correlative which
represents the height of cinema. Every thought in her mind
is clearly visible, every feeling. The undoubted bias is towards
the woman and Madhabi Mukerjee in particular, for in her
Ray found the embodiment of a certain type of Indian woman
just as he had found the man in Soumitra Chatterjee. Deeply
intelligent, sensitive, outwardly graceful, self-composed and
serene but inwardly the kind of traditional Indian woman
of today whose inner seismograph catches the vibration waves
reaching from outside into her seclusion, stirring her with a
spiritual unrest. The world outside her window is changing,

and down in the drawing room the Mill-Bentham-Rammohan Roy combination is inevitably working towards the liberation of woman.

Mahanagar is a contemporary story, and *Charulata* is a 'period-piece'. Yet in the later, the woman is more self-aware, and one might even call her ruthless. If her conscience does not trouble her too much, it is not merely because of her innocence; she has a strong character, she finds out what she wants and the knowledge does not shock her, it only makes her go forward to get her man. She reminds me, remotely, of Lady Macbeth in Wajda's Siberian film. In a society which tells a woman, 'here is the man that thou shalt love', she does not shy away from an impossible relationship; and, I repeat, this is only partly due to the innocent nature of her self-awareness. It does come to her so slowly that it is hard for her to draw the line; but in that unforgettable swing scene, she perceives the dark truth, without a shadow of doubt. Another 'transparent' moment, and a great one at that.

In the Tagore story, Bhupati goes away, at least for a while. He offers to take her with him, perhaps thinking that it might help restore their relationship; but after a moment's hesitation, Charu decides against it, Tagore takes the bold line of a firm spiritual break. Ray reunites them, in a series of 'freeze' shots, holding them in a suspended animation more true to real life. Perhaps the cinema, being more of a mass medium, stays behind literature in the expression of minority attitudes. It is not seen in the privacy of the individual's sanctum sanctorum; it offers a sharing of experience with a multitude of unknown entities. While that enriches the experience, it also makes it difficult to identify with the screen all by oneself. In the present stage of our middle-class society, the Tagore ending, with its symbolism of a final break, is unreal especially in a medium which presents thoughts and feelings through very immediate and concrete images and sounds constituting the objective correlative of the mental processes. Ray's ending seems to me to be perfect; it emphasizes reality and heightens the poignancy while doing so.

I see in *Kapurush,* irrespective of the fact that it is a

somewhat sloppily made film by Ray's and *Charulata's* standards, continuation of the theme of the woman's quest for happiness of her own making She is the same character, as self-possessed and serene as ever; but she has herself changed, through her previous experiences, as it were, in *Mahanagar* and *Charulata*. She tasted economic independence in the first, and wanted it; in the second she found the man she loved, and longed for the right to go on loving him. In *Kapurush* she is the woman who has lost both. She is married to a vapid tea-planter whom she never loved; she stays married to him because that is the only way for a woman, even in the bulk of upper crust society. She is almost in the same state of suspended animation as she was at the end of *Charulata*. And suddenly, to disturb her peace, her earlier love reappears on the scene. She knows already that he failed once to take her away out of everything as the real man of her secret dreams would (she only relives the experience in the flashback where, as a modern woman, she can express her need to the extent of vocalising it and offering marriage on a platter); and she knows that he will fail again, only this time, it is not out of any noble sentiment for a brother, but out of inability to defy society. Again her character is much more eloquent in its silence than of the others with their long speeches. Again, the director's mind is concentrated on the woman's aspect of the situation. *Kapurush* is thus a weaker re-statement of the same proposition and its importance lies only in the continuity of the theme and the sense of finality which it brings to it. With increased freedom for the woman, the present system of marriage has proved inadequate and in Western society it shows signs of cracking up. Whether that is a good thing or not, let the social philosophers ponder. But the inescapable fact is that such pressures are beginning to be felt in our country with the progress in women's education and economic independence. It may well be that the director never thought consciously of such a continuity. But the fact is that it is clearly discernible.

It is typical of Ray that the most contemporary and the truest statement of the theme should be achieved in the exquisite period piece rather than in the garish contemporary

5

setting. In the first place contemporaneity is not something that belongs to the story of a film, but to the outlook the director brings to bear on it. If that had not been so, and if Shakespeare's plays had not been presented in manifold ways which evoke very contemporary responses in us, only the most determined students of English literature would go to see them today or even read them. Ray's contemplative, serene and lyrical style is symptomatic of a remoteness from the immediate problems of the day. The evolution in his heroes and his heroines which we have discussed shows that he is a chronicler of change in the main body of the Indian tradition. He does not throw himself with ardour into problems affecting small minorities which seem over-real to us when we belong to them. If he had not been able to stand back and look at what has happened in our country in the last hundred years, he could not have made the trilogy, or projected the Tagore era, the nineteenth-century Bengal renaissance, so completely and taken in even the fringe of the post-Tagore period.

III

It is not for nothing that Truffaut walked out of a showing of *Pather Panchali;* it was because he could not bear the slow rhythm. Arriving in a rush to see *Postmaster* once, I was irritated beyond measure by the time Anil Chatterjee took to turn his head less than 180 degrees. But, slowly, the film cast its spell; one was lifted out of the breathless pace of middle-class city life and placed in the heart of Indian reality, surrendering to the rhythm of life as it is lived by the majority of people and has been, for hundreds of years. The water-logged path, the little hut surrounded by bamboo groves become real; every movement of a face takes on meaning, becomes a personal experience. Yet Ray does not nostalgically idealize traditional India. The postmaster cannot stick the life in the village, and must go back; he is too city-bred. Apu moves from his village to Banaras and finally to Calcutta, inexorably drawn towards a wider, more modern world. *Jalsaghar* records the decay of feudalism, no matter with how much melancholy; *Debi* gently points to the protest against superstition naturally arising out of scientific education. Amulya in *Samapti* sports the portrait of Napoleon and wears tartan socks and the Oxford shoes which become the occasion for so much amusement due to their unsuitability for the village, and the piquancy created by the wayward mixture of tradition and modernity.

In India, the hiatus between the modern and the traditional, the educated and the uneducated, the rich and the poor is so great that this process of identification with the rhythm and the reality of the life of the people (even if it does not stretch far beyond the middle class) is essential to any art which is not prepared to be ephemeral. The rhythm of Ray's films is one of the finest things about his work for the very reason that it expresses a wider reality than the one that we are used to in our islands of modernity in India.

It is also intimately bound up with the contemplative nature of his style, the preoccupation with what happens in the mind rather than on the surface level. His work abounds in long wordless passages in which his characters do very little and express a great deal. Think, for instance, of the long, slow opening shot of *Jalsaghar* showing the old man sitting out on the terrace in the twilight, his back to the camera, and his servant reaching him the end of his long pipe. It sets the keynote of the entire film — the sense of the passing away of an old order, of the twilight not only of his own life, but of an age. For those who look upon the cinema as vehicle of action and drama, Ray's work is anti-film. In the one sequence of *Jalsaghar* in which he essays a sudden spirit of dramatic action — the death by drowning of his son and his wife — he is acutely uncomfortable and becomes almost banal both in the symbol of the upturned boat and the manner of introduction of the dead boy. In *Jalsaghar* as well as in *Debi,* he takes a story with great 'dramatic' potential but underplays the element of conflict and highlights the element of contemplation. Perhaps he feels, like Auguste Renoir, that 'the hero portrayed at the moment when he is defying the enemy, or a woman shown in the hardest pain of labour, is not a suitable subject for a great painting, though men and women who have passed through such ordeals and been ennobled by them become great subjects when later on the artist can portray them in repose. It is not the transitory character of an individual which should be fixed in marble, the culmination of his entire life, heroic or cowardly, commonplace or fascinating. In short, the artist's task is not to stress this or that *instant* [italics mine] in a human being's existence, but to make comprehensible the man in his entirety' (*Renoir, My Father,* by Jean Renoir, Collins, 1962).

The inevitability and the direction of change is never in doubt in *Jalsaghar* or *Debi;* that is why Ray is content to express the individual in his entirety and never feels the need to take up the cudgel for social reform. In *Debi,* he has no less sympathy for the father-in-law who becomes obsessed with the idea that his son's wife is the incarnation of the goddess, than for the unfortunate girl who gives her life for it. To Ray, both are victims, one of his superstition, and the other of the consequences of it. There is no anger, no sense of urgency in settling burning issues and no obvious partisanship for the forces of change.

In this sense of resignation and fatality, Ray is Indian to the core. Indian tradition views existence as a continuous line of epic sweep rather than as a tight circle of drama in which death brings tragedy. The Apu trilogy is almost as littered with dead bodies as *Hamlet,* yet the feeling is totally different. Durga dies, followed by Harihar, and then Sarbajaya; finally Aparna. But life goes on, and hope never dies. The 'tragic view of life' of Western literature is totally absent in Ray.

In today's India hope is not just an eternal tradition; it is here and now. The country is in the midst of awakening and change. A vast process of change has been taking place for more than a hundred years with the impact of Western scientific thought on an ancient civilization. Until independence, it was largely confined to the educated middle class, but since a faster tempo of industrialization set in, it has begun to spread even to the masses of the people. The poorest or the most sceptical Indian realises today that although material prosperity and the modern age are not waiting round the corner, India cannot remain in its present condition for ever. Perhaps in the past hope had something to do with the hereafter or at most with the imminence of Independence; now it springs from the aspiration towards a better life in this world. Dialectically enough, the hope of material prosperity produces a sense of faith; and faith is an important element in art. Ray's work does not merely record the poverty of India; it is imbued with hope, and faith in the human being, one of the corner-stones of the Tagore philosophy.

The spiritual restlessness of a Bergman or a Fellini or a Kurosawa lies in the search for the hope and faith which they cannot find. Inevitably, the difference in spirit gives rise to differences in form. We have already seen how the slow tempo of Ray's films reflects the rhythm of life in India and brings about a deeper sense of Indian reality. In that respect, it is very different from the slow rhythm of an Antonioni which demands a response which is not 'natural' to the Western way of life today, but rather runs counter to it and therefore creates bitter controversies. Ray's images are what I would call 'musical' in expressiveness (not unlike Antonioni's); their evocation sends out ripples far beyond the conscious understanding created by the elements making up the image. They are 'decorative', pronouncedly so as in *Charulata,* but to varying degrees in other films as well. This, too, is embedded in the Indian tradition in which 'decoratif' is not a word of abuse as in France. In Rajasthani miniatures or classical music, decoration and expression are one and the same thing. The deliberateness of Satyajit's composition does not inhibit the spontaneity of the work which flows like Indian music, improvising freely within some very broad definitions. Even his background music often becomes memorable by itself, as in *Pather Panchali* or in *Charulata,* and is not the 'unheard music' that background music in films is ideally supposed to be. The melodic themes are often recognisable and memorable and emphasize the lyrical decorative aspects of his work.

The elements of his technique naturally derive a great deal from the West. There is the language of the silent, purely image-based cinema developed by the Russians; the French preoccupation with the individual; and the Italian neorealist manner of the silent spectator who sees the life of the individual flowing not in the isolation of drama (as in the French films of the thirties), but realistically through the surrounding *indifference* of life in general. From the first he removes the abstractness of montage; from the second, its restless, endless conversation and the dramatic isolation of the protagonists; and from the third, its theoretical and excessively conscious repudiation of the story. But it is his Indianness that fuses all he derives into a form entirely his own. And it is his deep identification with a region — which he has maintained with a ruthless integrity — that results in the universal appeal of his work.

A quality which Ray shares with important directors elsewhere is the intensely personal vision and apprehension in his work. To him the film could not be anything but the director's medium. He scripts all his films and now writes the music for them as well. On all aspects of his films he exercises complete control, having very clear ideas of his exact requirement in every piece of lighting, camera movement, editing or art direction. To make doubly sure, he works always with the same group of technicians so that his way of working and his intentions are completely understood. It is only in the case of acting that this degree of control varies according to the actor's ability to create what the director wants. When he deals with non-professionals or new finds he often creates the entire acting by dictating every gesture; the expressiveness and mobility of face become his actor's sole contribution. Ray achieves this severe process of integration and subordination of the contributions of many in a very free and natural manner far removed from the straitjacketing which my remarks seem to suggest. Today his unit is like a well-oiled machine which moves easily under his hand and gives him his facility of expression. But it was in the days, or rather years, of *Pather Panchali* when this instrument was forged through an enormous struggle with internal and external forces. The film lay incomplete for months together for lack of money until the West Bengal Government came forward with help. Throughout this long period, Ray was able to hold his personal vision of the film intact and to bring it out in his work, which from the early scripting to the final print must have taken about three years. To sustain the purity and force of an inspiration for so long in the distracting medium of the cinema, and to deliver it intact in the final result is itself the evidence not only of great creative energy but of the intensely personal character of creativity.

In *Pather Panchali,* Ray created his basic style and technique. It was not without its rough edges (think of the sequence of Durga's illness with its element of theatrical contrivance), but the truth of inspiration carried it along. In *Aparajito,* his technique becomes more mature and polished and capable of infinite subtlety. Less obvious emotions now become capable of expression with more restraint (as in the death of Sarbajaya). In *Jalsaghar* he made his first important attempt in the studio with a professional actor and complex resources of his problems. *Jalsaghar* is the most outstanding example of his technique till *Charulata* — in his handling of a vast set, mixing the real and artificial — and significantly, it came out of the oldest and most primitive of Calcutta's studios. In the terrace scene of its opening, the moonlit verandah sequence, the music-hall in session, the ride to death, every shade of feeling and atmosphere is brought out with great subtlety and becomes the very stuff of cinema. For sheer atmosphere and mood, it is hard to find the equal of *Jalsaghar,* and it is because of the dominance of these two elements that craftsmanship plays such an important role in the film. From here on Ray is completely sure of himself and uses the camera almost with the fluency of a writer using his pen. To master technique and to subordinate it completely to one's will is the first requirement of personal artistic expression, and in the cinema it often becomes the number one enemy because of its enormous complexities and temptations. Watching him shooting *Teen Kanya,* I was struck by this fluency of perfect technique — the result of many years of work.

It is not the perfection of technique, however, that makes Ray's films important. Their hope and faith and their complete Indianness reflected most of all in their un-Western rhythm exercise their fascination on us as well as the Western world. The revelation — to Venice — of *Aparajito,* and the Catholic award to *Charulata* are fully symptomatic of this. As

I have tried to establish earlier, the world and the mind he projects is basically of the Bengal renaissance, of the mythology and typology of the Tagore era.   In a way he is a chronicler of the past; yet the inner assurance of hope and faith which this brings out in his films is not a thing of the past, for these feelings are buried under the surface in contemporary India in the Nehru dream, and justifies, for once, one of *Time* magazine's glib aphorisms which describes the Apu trilogy as the 'Mahabharata of Modern India'.   Although it derives from an ethos embodied in past literature and thought, it becomes symbolic of the present in a larger-than-life manner on a wide canvas of India over a historic period.   Nehru stood somewhere between Gandhiji and Tagore; and the truth of the Tagore value-world never quite lost its appeal in Nehru's India. In fact it found new expression in the ideals, if not in all the realities of the Nehru era.

IV

The Calcutta of the burning trams, the communal riots, the refugees, unemployment, the rising prices and the food shortage do not exist in Ray's films.   Although he lives in this city, there is no correspondence between him and the poetry of anguish which dominates Bengali literature of the day and has done since Jibanananda Das.   The trials of the sensitive mind trying to survive the excruciating pressure of corruption, vulgarity, want and total pointlessness find no echo in him.   On the whole, he has portrayed the past evolution of the middle class as reflected in the long period dominated by Tagore.   It is something that has gone into the making of himself and his generation; something that he knows and understands.   In a broad way, it forms the background of his experience.   The experience need not necessarily be directly personal; the people, the mores, the times, the attitudes reflected in the Tagore era's literature become, through repetition and constant explanation, part of the fabric of personal experience.   A certain image of the villager, the young man getting to know the world outside and turning into the ardent social reformer, the women slowly liberated through education and the social evolution brought

Cover of the first issue of Indian Film Culture, published by the Federation of the Film Societies

Still from Calcutta Film Society's Production— Portrait of a City

Jean Renoir speaking at the Calcutta Film Society

Chidananda Das Gupta speaking at a Calcutta Film Society reception for Pudovkin (2nd from left)

Lalita Pawar in Jagirdar's Ramshastri

Uday Shankar &
Amala in Kalpana

Pramathesh Barua with Jamuna in his Devdas   Balraj Sahani in Bimal Roy's Do Bigha Zamin

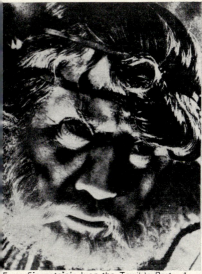

From Eisenstein's Ivan the Terrible Part—1

From Akira Kurosawa's Rashomon

From Fellini's La strada

Chaplin : The Kid

From De Sica's Bicycle Thieves

From Ingmar Bergman's Seventh Seal

From Antonioni's L' Avventura

From Grigori Chukhrai's Forty First.

From Milos Forman's
Loves of a Blonde

Supriya Chowdhury in Ritwik Ghatak's Meghe Dhaka Tara

Madhabi Mukherjee in Satyajit Ray's Charulata
ali Banerjee and Kajal in Ritwik Ghatak's Ajantrik

Madhabi in Mrinal Sen's Baishe Shravan

Utpal Dutta in Mrinal Sen's
Bhuban Shome

Shashi Kapoor and Mousumi
Chatterjee in Anari

Vinode Khanna in Kachche Dhaage

about by the Brahmo movement crystallizes in the poems, plays, stories, novels and essays not only of Tagore but of the writers of his period; and it is this image which projects itself in Ray's films. Hence it is that Ray's characters are powerfully simplified and contained within very broad outlines of the typology of the period.

The Soumitra-Madhabi roles, the Bhupati of *Charulata,* the landlord of *Jalsaghar,* the clerk of *Parash Pathar* all follow this main direction. It is a kind of apprehension of character which tends to fall down when it deals with characters more or less unfamiliar to this typology, as in the capitalist of *Jalsaghar,* the tea-planter of *Kapurush,* partly even in the rising woman of *Mahanagar.* The idealism of the Tagore period often underplayed the unpleasant truths of character, the contradictory urges inevitable to human beings. The biographies of this period, for instance, never bring out the man in his total psychology; they select the more pleasant, publicly displayable traits. Tagore himself never reveals his personal life in the way of Gandhiji. Gandhiji was not a Brahmo, and his outlook was not contained within the framework of the rise of the middle class in India. At its best the Tagore trend resulted in the emergence of noble images of character; at its worst, it was full of hypocrisy, a little puritan, a little afraid of Freud, and shied away from ugliness. It was never suited to the depiction of life in the raw, of showing the facets of character that are shocking to behold. The furthest it goes in revealing human weakness is in the delicate and forgiving treatment of it in *Charulata.*

The novels of Manik Bandyopadhyay, for instance, show life in all its violence, its aberrations, its ugliness and the sheer animal force of evil which motivates much of society. Tagore or Bibhuti Bhushan or even Tarashankar Banerjee would not touch such things with kid gloves. Neither these more terrible aspects of our society, nor the poetry of anguish generated by the struggle of the 'Ravindriks' to cope with them are reflected in Ray's films. In fact wherever he has taken a tentative step towards them, Ray has tended to burn his fingers. Take *Abhijan* for instance; the attempt to enter the underworld of the working class results in total failure. And the reason for the failure is that it cannot be drawn from the myths and types of the Tagore world. To see the extent of the failure, one can compare it to the poetic yet stark reality of say *La strada*. One is not surprised to hear that the film was originally to have been made by someone else from a script by Ray, and that at the last moment he decided to take it on. Even the atmosphere of the office in which the Arati of *Mahanagar* works is just not complex enough; it never exudes quite the dankness, the monumental indifference, the cynicism and self-seeking which make up the fabric of such inelegant reality. It is strenuously woven, and the clear-cut characters and individuals in the office situation carry no suggestion of unseen depths. The powerful simplifications of his earlier-period films tend towards over-simplification. In other words Ray fails to enter the post-Tagore world in which the young idealist has either turned cynic or has turned away from partriotism, politics and social reform, even the pioneering of business (Subhas Chandra was Mayor of the Corporation and P. C. Roy the founder of the pharmaceutical industry), because all of this proves too dirty to him and makes him take refuge in the 'poetry of anguish'.

It is a moot question as to whether the later generation brought up by Tagore in the pre-Independence era of hope, was toughened enough in its training to cope with the pressures of stark reality released by the disillusion, greed, corruption, and ruthless behaviour in the post-Independence era. The idealist of our days must be made of much sterner stuff, capable of holding his own against evil. Even the rural scene today has changed; the typology of the past no longer fits. The image of village life conjured up for long by literary habits has finally become untrue. New types are being created by the incursion of planned investment into the countryside, the invasion of the radio, the block development offices, family planning drives, the commercial cinema, the money generated by soaring food prices and the price-support policy of the government, the opening up of communications. The myths of the Tagore era are no longer adequate to express the complex change in attitudes in the India that is taking shape today. They provide a rich background to the middle class mind but it is painfully clear

that the translation and the advancement of these values into
a tougher outlook and language are necessary.

The post-Tagore age has finally caught up with us. It is an
age that might call for a passionate involvement, ruthless
exposure of hypocrisies of the past and the present, and the
exploration of a new synthesis of wider dimensions on the part
of the artist. The film is an art which, willy-nilly, must reflect
these changes in social reality in some way or the other. Whether
Ray will enter into a new phase of development to do so or
new artists will arise out of these new and less serene urges
of the times, it is impossible to say. Or will the most significant expression of intellect and sensibility — which in the
years of Ray in Bengal has been the domain of the cinema —
move to another medium ?

1965

Bengali cinema: in and out of the Ray umbrella

For the major part of some two hundred years of British rule in India, Calcutta was the capital of the country. It was thus the main focus, for a long time, of India's contact with the West. Closeness to the seat of power gave the Bengali a certain advantage over people from other parts of the country, mainly in the educational-cultural area. Bengal was quick to put these advantages to use in furthering the development of the country; people like Raja Rammohan Roy opted for a Western education in the sciences and the humanities as the best course of progress for India. This brought about, in Bengal to begin with, an urge for social change and a contemporary outlook.

Compared to many other parts of India, Bengal was never rich in tradition. Oriya prose, for instance, is some two hundred and fifty years older than the Bengali. Nothing like Tulsidas's Ramayana with its deep-flowing influence on the thoughts of millions of people all over Northern India was written in Bengali. The Bengalis originated from aboriginal tribes blended with Mongolians and Aryans. By contrast, the people of Uttar Pradesh or *Aryavarta* in middle North India which became, with constant invasions in the further northwest, the refuge of purist Aryan culture, have a far richer historical tradition. Having much to conserve, they became conservative. Having little to lose, the Bengalis embraced the thinking of the British, although not so much their outward ways, much more quickly. Through the British, contact developed with a good part of Europe, particularly France and Germany, sometimes with other parts of the world. As a result, the outlook in Bengali culture became, and has remained, the most contemporary in India.

Raja Rammohan Roy was deeply stirred by the French Revolution and kept in active contact with social movements all over Europe. Social-reformist demands for the abolition of idolatry, child marriage, polygamy, the burning of the widows, superstitions about crossing the sea (*kalapani*), discrimination against women, and so on expressed themselves most forcefully in this area, particularly in the shape of the Brahmo Samaj movement, and became effective well before the middle of the nineteenth century. The cultural effect of this was later evident in the work of the Tagores. Their contact with the West was so close that barely two years after the Bauhaus group was formed in Germany in 1919, they held an exhibition of Bauhaus art in Calcutta. Chinese, Japanese and Balinese painting were major influences on the philosopher-poet Rabindranath Tagore and were evident in Vishva-Bharati or 'World-University', which he founded at Shantiniketan, and in the Bengal school which flourished there. Bengali culture responded instantly to every intellectual impulse from abroad, whether it was the Russian Revolution or the Spanish Civil War, the poetry of T. S. Eliot, the prose of Marcel Proust. Considerable volumes of French and German literature had been translated into Bengali before the nineteenth century was out. The bulk of Bengali literature of the last one hundred years or more could not have been written without this living contact with the West, and a constant synthesis of tradition with modernity. In the nineteenth century and early twentieth century a great deal of scholarship in Sanskrit, Persian and Arabic was combined with the study of Western philosophy and literature. It is doubtful whether both in form and content, better contemporary poetry has been written in modern India than the works of Jibanananda Das, Sudhindranath Datta and Bishnu De, which range so freely across Indian and Western literature, both classical and modern. The impecunious Bengali middle class also represents, very probably, the largest single group of culturally responsive people in the country.

This openness to impulses from abroad helped Bengal in assimilating the new medium of the cinema into its predominantly literary fold. Despite the somewhat chauvinistic claims made by Bengalis on behalf of the half-mythical Hiralal Sen, the cinema was pioneered in Maharashtra. The accent, however, was on the mythological and the spectacular, with little sense of the contemporary and, still less, a grasp of this technological medium born out of Western industrial society. D. G. Phalke, the great pioneer, devoted himself entirely to mythology; the Marathi cinema which followed him had a greater socio-historical awareness, but its concepts, generally speaking, stayed close to a traditional and theatrical character. The Bengali cinema, from the days of D. G. (Dhiren Ganguly) took to contemporary subjects — D. G.'s own first film *Bilet-Pherat* ('Foreign-Returned') — although 'devotional' pictures were also produced. It was Himangshu Rai who let in a breath of fresh air into the cobwebs of Bombay's till then traditional use of a modern medium through his collaboration with the German, Franz Osten, and international films like *Light of Asia* (1925) and *Karma* (1933). P. C. Barua in Bengal brought about a more modern Indian, progressive outlook and sophistication in the handling of the medium with *Debdas* (1935) and *Mukti* (1937). *Debdas* glorifies the dropout lover and the prostitute; *Mukti*'s hero frees his wife from her social bondage to him so that she can marry another. Barua's cinematic ingenuity matured the style of Bengali cinema and left a stamp of seriousness on its content. Debdas became an archetypal hero who still serves as the model for much film writing. Dilip Kumar, the doyen of film actors in India, became what he did only after playing the title role of *Debdas* (in the later Hindi remake) which left an indelible mark, not only on himself, but on virtually all film acting in the commercial cinema. Guru Dutt, the most sensitive of the middle generation film directors of the talkie era in Bombay, gives evidence of a very deep Bengali influence and was in fact a sort of spiritual successor to Barua. Bimal Roy, who did not share Guru Dutt's cinematic sensibility, made a success of a genre of films with the Bengali type of 'clean content' and sentimental appeal in Bombay. In his *Do Bigha Zamin* (1953), the first half displayed a much greater cinematic sensibility than all his other films.

But we Bengalis love to talk. Also to write. The power of the word, spoken or written, has fascinated us for a long time. For nearly a century, universities have churned out graduates by the thousands who still fill the cafés with cigarette smoke and political talk. The partition of Bengal in 1905 was rescinded largely because of the eloquence of people like Surendranath Banerjea. There are few young men of my generation who at some time or the other did not write poetry. As the late Ramananda Chatterjee, a puritan and upright journalist if ever there was one, said so tersely : 'Everybody has the measles at least once; everybody writes poetry at least once, especially when he is young.'

This love of words has coloured the Bengali's attitude to the other arts. The music which, until recently, most attracted the Bengali has been set to words—the *kirtan, baul* and other philosophical-folk forms and, by way of classical music, the Bishnupur *gharana* in *dhrupad* which itself lays some emphasis on words. It was only in recent times that classical instrumental music rose to its heights with Ravi Shanker, Ali Akbar, Vilayet Khan, Nikhil Banerjee, Pannalal Ghosh and others. Dancing has never been our forte. The classical styles have never really taken root. The Bengal school of painting was also literary and descriptive in character. Bengali theatre was founded by a Russian, Gerashim Lebedeff, and grew into the traditions of the Victorian English stage until changes were signalled in the work of the so-called non-professionals like Shambhu Mitra, Utpal Dutta and others. It was perhaps its heavy literary inheritance which prevented the emergence of the cinematic idiom in Bengal in spite of its contemporary outlook.

Unlike literature and the fine arts, Bengali cinema was isolated from world trends and had no acquaintance with any foreign cinema other than Hollywood and Britain. Hollywood cannot be imitated by any film industry without its resources, and Britain was not worth imitating. Except for Barua, hardly anyone had been exposed to any worthwhile experience abroad. With an impractical model in Hollywood, the Bengali love for song, and the penchant for theatre, Bengali cinema produced a peculiar combination of poor Hollywood, half-baked literature, a load of songs, and some poor dancing.

At one stroke, Satyajit Ray took the wordiness out of Bengali cinema — in his own work. The contemporary bias of the Bengali mind, always seeking a synthesis between tradition and modernity à la Tagore, found expression in the natural medium of a technological age. His films instantly became the most Indian and the most cinematic expression ever achieved in the country. Ray's concern for humanity transcends national boundaries and evokes sympathetic vibrations among sensitive people throughout the world. This humanism is a direct product of Tagorean-Gandhian compassion which rises above national and partisan considerations in a country that is, in spite of its spectacular progress in many directions, still the scene of some of the most gruesome poverty in the world affecting the majority of its population. Ray has sometimes been criticised for showing India's poverty abroad. But in his universal vision, the poverty or fatalism of an Indian somehow turns into the silent suffering of all mankind. His work is of value to India and to the world as a reminder of the state of the have-not, whether it is the Brahmin family of the trilogy, or the innocent girl caught in the web of man-made divinity in *Debi,* or the lonely wife who finds love outside marriage in *Charulata.*

Neither of the two outstanding figures of the Bengali cinema other than Ray can be said to have been influenced by him; yet it is doubtful if their work would have been possible without his example and impact. Ritwik Ghatak's first film, *Nagarik,* made in 1953 but not released bears the full imprint of his Marxist faith and his IPTA (Indian People's Theatre Association) involvement, but not an identity with the film medium. *Ajantrik,* coming two years after *Pather Panchali* leaps into a valid individual form and a completely cinematic idiom. Ray seems to have acted as a catalyst. The story of the taxi driver who bears an almost human love for the battered car he drives and refuses to change for something new, is really an essay on the acceptance of the machine into the mental make-up of an ancient agricultural country. The opening sequences of the lunatic bridegroom's drive across rain-swept hills and forests are unforgettable.* But some of the connections he seeks to make between tribal dancing and the decrepit old car with its obsessed driver remain arbitrary and obscure in spite of the film-maker's own fascinating explanations.

Ghatak's three films on the theme of the refugees from East Pakistan — *Meghe Dhaka Tara* (1959), *Komal Gandhar* (1960) and *Subarnarekha* (1965) —form a powerful trilogy of which the first piece is the best integrated. Here, Ghatak establishes his characters and situations with great conviction; unlike what he did in *Ajantrik,* he uses a lot of dialogue because his story needs it. Vocal music is beautifuly woven into the story and is an integral part of it. For once, one does not feel it is a trick to introduce some songs into a film. In fact, the singing sets the moods of hope and despair, of the force of life itself. The musical brother and the girl who steals her elder sister's lover through her animal magnetism, stand out sharp and clear. In contrast the ending, with its strident cry 'I want to live', does not quite make the leap into a larger dimension which the film-maker seems to have sought.

Of the other two films on this theme, *Komal Gandhar* suffers from an obsessive effort to interpolate and convert literary ideas and images directly into the film medium, the beginnings of which had already been seen in *Meghe Dhaka Tara* (for example, the sound of the whiplash when the elder sister retreats after discovering her younger sister with her lover). The Miranda-Sita-Shakuntala comparisons are too literary, the convolutions of the infighting within the theatre too dependent on the audience's knowledge of the evolution of the Indian People's Theatre Association for the film to attain any universality. Ghatak, the cinéaste and Ghatak the writer of some forty short stories and several plays seem to fall into

---

* The taxi driver, played superbly by Kali Banerjee, is a far more credible character than that played by Soumitra Chatterjee in Ray's *Abhijan,* whose upper middle class identity is hardly concealed by beard and turban. The picture of Ghatak's driver, seated under a tree near a tank with the decrepit old car standing in the distance, and breaking into a religious song in his stentorian voice is unforgettable. The whole atmosphere around the repair and running of the car, the conversations with people, the outbursts of a mad man are much more convincing and indicate a more intimate knowledge of the milieu than Ray displays in his film.

6

two compartments. Yet there are sudden flashes of cinematic splendour as when he shows the end of the railway track pointing at the river that divides West Bengal from East Bengal or when his camera sweeps with his much-favoured wide-angle lens the panorama of the great river darkened by clouds. The film is marred only by the sudden and undisciplined outbursts of literary-sentimental expression. Ghatak seems often unable to find the apt objective correlative of his passions and to lack the patience to seek them out. As a result the film would probably be almost incomprehensible to a non-Bengali audience, not to speak of a non-Indian audience.

His erratic genius is most evident in *Subarnarekha*. In a film of striking situation — the sequences of the abandoned wartime airstrip and the drunken revelry of the disillusioned refugee intellectuals in a restaurant — he is so disconcertingly without a sense of characterisation, particularly in the central role played by Abhi Bhattacharya, that one is left wondering how he achieved it so well in *Meghe Dhaka Tara*. At the same time, it must be said to the everlasting credit of Ghatak that when he sets down his camera to face the Bengal countryside, he does not remind us at all of Ray, but creates something entirely of his own, as in the airstrip sequence and shots of the river. The scene of the once-revolutionary brother in search of a prostitute, discovering his own sister as one, which leads to her suicide, shows a strength of passion which enables Ghatak to approach action frontally, if melodramatically. This is in contrast to Ray who approaches obliquely and who is more interested in the effect of action than in action itself and sometimes is in difficulty when the frontal approach becomes unavoidable. *Meghe Dhaka Tara,* more than *Subarnarekha,* bears evidence of Ghatak's ability to draw great performances out of his actors. Supriya Chowdhury is a different actress when working with Ghatak than with any other director. As the singing hero of *Meghe Dhaka Tara,* Anil Chatterjee too turns in a performance unequalled in his career for its passionate sincerity.

Ghatak's compulsive concern with the present and his approach to action set him apart from Ray; yet the polarity can be over-stressed, because both share a Tagore heritage, and Ghatak had his share of faith in certain universal values not overly different from Ray's. Indeed some of the turbulence of his life may have proceeded from his attempt to reconcile these Tagorean verities with his urgent revolutionary passions. He has been much celebrated as the *enfant terrible* of Bengali cinema and held up as a sort of anti-Ray hero. Perhaps this is so more because of his verbal pronouncements than his work whose sense of values is much closer to Ray's than one is at first led to believe. He is deeply rooted in tradition; in *Meghe Dhaka Tara* the elder sister is compared to Uma, Mahadeva's consort, *Komal Gandhar* keeps harking back to Kalidas and *Subarnarekha* to the Upanishads. His film on the Chhow dancers of Purulia is not very different from what one would have expected Ray to make of it; only the short on Lenin (shown in the USSR but not in India) by dint of its subject and its characteristically direct approach to action, strikes one as different. In terms of the basic values cherished by the two, the difference is not as great as it seems.

In an interview given to extreme leftist groups in Bangladesh, Ghatak says: 'No national art can be built without reclaiming tradition with the help of science.' Accused of using classical music and Tagore music with their 'class character' he retorted: 'All art work is class work; it is all class-based, whether in China or in the Soviet Union. I shall use classical music in the contemporary context, in spite of its class moorings, because I need it.' He was stung to the quick when criticised for not providing 'revolutionary solutions' : 'I don't consider slogan-mongering and prescribing solutions to be my task at all.... If I can present the problem before people, that is enough.' He protested that *Subarnarekha* had no sense of decadence or despair in it, much as Satyajit Ray would in the case of *Debi* or *Jalsaghar*.

Like Ray, he controlled all aspects of film-making, writing his own scripts, making his own camera set-ups and compositions, breathing down the neck of his editor and dictating every single cut. Although he never composed his own music, he had a fine ear for it, and collaborated effectively with well-known musicians — Ali Akbar Khan in *Ajantrik*, Jyotirindra Moitra (of IPTA fame) in *Komal Gandhar* and *Meghe Dhaka*

Tara. Here it should be recalled that before coming to the cinema, Ghatak had been deeply involved with the IPTA, which was a potent force in the revitalization of all art in that period and left an indelible mark on Bengali as also in Indian drama.

In contrast to Ray and Ghatak, it is Mrinal Sen, the only other outstanding figure in contemporary Bengali cinema, who seems to be free from traditional concerns and problems of their reconciliation with the present. He lives altogether in the present, specially in his later work.

Slower than Ghatak in his evolution towards individuality, Mrinal Sen served a long apprenticeship in the film industry before making his first, and rather pedestrian, film, *Raat-Bhor* (1955; released two months after *Pather Panchali*) which showed little promise of his later achievements. *Nil Akasher Nichay* (1959), based on a Mahadevi Verma story of a Chinese hawker in India (in the halcyon days of 'Hindi-Chini bhai-bhai'), made its mark in the box office and set Mrinal Sen firmly on his long road to distinction. With a fine performance from Kali Banerjee as the Chinaman, the film had a novel subject and a clear, if undistinguished style of story-telling. It is his next film, *Baishe Sraban* (1960) that found Sen drawn to the slow rhythm and the lyrical naturalism of Ray. The film has a certain poignancy and humour, and its idiom is completely cinematic. It owes little to pre-*Pather Panchali* Bengali cinema. The handling of action in the famine sequence, the scene of the storm at the fair, the train sequence — all have a grasp of *mise en scène* and a direct-ness, again rather different from Ray's approach to action. There is also a greater sense of direct knowledge of lower middle class life; the characters are not taken from established literary types and brought to life as in Ray — they are more directly perceived and derived from reality. Sen's years as a medical salesman must have stood him in good stead in the casting and dialogue of, say the early scenes of *Baishe Sraban.* But the psychological drama between the husband, irascible in his enforced idleness, and the sensitive wife unable to cope with him, is pitched too ambitiously and falls far short of its promise. The wife's suicide is perhaps for this reason, curiously ineffective (compare with any of the deaths in the Apu trilogy).

Thematically allied to this, but far less successful, is *Punash-cha* (1961) which scratches the surface of the problem of the economic independence of a wife, handled with much greater depth by Ray in *Mahanagar* (1963). In fact, with the exception of the first half of *Abasheshe* (1963), this period in Sen's work seems to be one of a search for identity, a groping for style and statement which the director could call his own. *Pratinidhi* (1964) suffers from the same rather listless casting about for vaguely progressive themes — in this case the re-marriage of a widow with a son — while a vaguely explora-tory camera looks around for a style. Only in *Abasheshe* does Sen blossom forth with a great comic flair which he appears to have so far suppressed for reasons best known to him. The first half has a refreshing, uninhibited capacity for fun and a sense of humour rare in the Indian cinema. The second half collapses into the worst quagmire of traditional-sentimental Bengali moviedom, turning this film into one of the most bizarre chapters of Sen's career.

Few film directors have been blessed with the mix of spon-taneity and deliberateness of Mrinal Sen. Soon after the script of *Akash-Kusum* by Ashish Burman was ready, Sen happened to see Truffaut's *Jules et Jim* at a showing of the Calcutta Film Society. Eureka ! He had found his style. *Akash-Kusum's* script was hastily rewritten and the freezes and jump-cuts must have curdled the blood of his editor. The film is one long Eureka shout — youthful, exuberant, and full of flourish. From here on, Sen never looked back. His progress towards a socia-list content couched in vigorous and inventive, if not always mature, terms was established, and became his hallmark. As he grows older, Mrinal Sen becomes more youthful in his love for the medium of the cinema and his need to play with it. So much so that sometimes the form overwhelms the content.

Yet it must be said in his defence that after the heady cham-pagne of *Akash-Kusum,* he steadied himself in *Matira Manisha* (1966). Its style still reflects the elements that Sen had so prodigally thrown around in *Akash-Kusum,* but the mirror is more placid, the gimmicks are timed with greater sophistication. He takes a fully contemporary view of a classic of Oriya literature, 1930, and brushes aside the conventions of stylistic simplicity in so-called simple village life. But the chief distinction of *Matira Manisha* lies not so much in its Nouvelle Vague overtures as in its flights of fancy and its sensitive perception of many of the scenes. The silent communication between the picture of a girl on a wall calendar and the young villager, and later the wild abandon of his young wife's dance at his provocation, are some of the finest love sequences seen in Indian cinema. Equally inventive and effective are the dream sequence in negative and the connection made between the mythical Garuda-like bird of the young man's dream and the wartime aeroplane he had seen during the day, probably for the first time in his life. The call of the outside world symbolized in this and other scenes, which alienates him from his elder brother, gives the film a different and an altogether contemporary flavour to Panigrahi's novel.

This interaction between the rural and urban worlds is reversed with much vitality and freshness in *Bhuban Shome* (1969) which forms another landmark in Mrinal Sen's progress. Its most remarkable aspect is the bizarre confrontation of two social classes that never really speak to each other : the educated upper class and the common man. Utpal Dutt's inimitable comic flair matches Sen's own to bring vividly to life the humanization of an uptight bureaucrat by the revelation of his own smallness, irrelevance and inadequacy in the face of the freshness and ease of the young girl. Suhasini Mulay is the embodiment of this innocence which transforms the strange man from the city. The bleak magnificence of the landscape plays no less a part. No wonder the portentious official finds it impossible to go back to his former pettiness and self-importance. Like Shome in the last sequence, the film too refuses to take itself too seriously. Its mix of fantasy and reality, of burlesque and serious drama, is delightful. Shome's bone-rattling cart ride, his running in fear of the domestic buffalo, his failure to shoot a single bird in all his hunting forays, contrasted with the naturalness of the girl and bound together by a bag of tricks taken out of the Nouvelle Vague cinema, give *Bhuban Shome* an even greater contem-

poraneity than *Matira Manisha*. The film can be faulted much
for its lack of narrative logic; but Sen has an airy way of
dismissing this logic with his flights of fancy. Shome's transformation is not organic enough, his encounter with the girl
has its touch of unreality, his pardon of her husband is too
directly the result of his meeting her, some of the sequences
are overlong. Its originality is nevertheless striking and its
humour infectious.

With this film, Sen's evolution reaches a high point, the
march towards which had begun with the technical raptures
of *Akash-Kusum*. His structuring is often lopsided, his
rhythm erratic (unlike Ray and Ghatak, he seems to have
little feeling for music), but one is left in no doubt about his
capacity to grow. And his persistent youthfulness reminds
one of Bazin on Renoir's fascination with the process of life
which often got the better of his storytelling intentions, but
gave his work its unfailing vitality.

Compared to Ray and Ghatak, Sen seems to belong more
definitely to a post-Tagore society and shows a freedom from
that value-world. Like them, he too is a puritan in matters
of sex. Man-woman relationships are handled with a look-
but-dont-touch attitude by all three. The sense of guilt in
this may be unrelated to the deep awareness of poverty which
their work reflects. There is, besides, a shared awareness of
the need and the inevitability of change, particularly between
Ray and Sen. In Ghatak, there is a greater sense of personal
agony as part of the agony of Bengal. In *Pather Panchali*,
there is a sense of discovery of the village and of poverty, an
urge to identify to which an urban audience in long servitude
of foreign rulers and raised partly within their culture, re-
sponds with a sense of homecoming.

Ghatak has none of this; he already belongs. If anything,
he belongs too much to stand apart from it and give it a universal meaning. Ray is sometimes accused of catering to the
foreigner. But his films are so intensely regional that they cannot be designed to appeal to the outsider; so in relating to
the regional reality, he does not lose himself in it. What he
really does is to maintain equal distance from foreigner and
Indian alike. His material happens to be Indian, but his state-

ment is about humanity. Mrinal Sen is in some ways the least Bengali of the three. Almost from the beginning he has an all-India (plus young-Europe) attitude about him which increases as time goes on (*Nil Akasher Nichay* was based on a Hindi story, *Matira Manisha* was made in Oriya, *Adhe Adhuray*, which I have not seen, and *Bhuban Shome* in Hindi).

Sen and Ghatak were both brought up, unlike Ray, under the IPTA umbrella. They have, as it were, a sense of moral obligation to carry on its work in their own field. In doing so, perhaps they tend to become a little schematic. There is also a tendency to very readily strike up attitudes and to take sides, especially true in some of Sen's films. They also have a spiritual affinity with a body of actors from those days— Gnyanesh Mukherjee, Kali Banerjee, Bijon Bhattacharya, Sobha Sen and others — that Ray does not feel. His own discoveries are Soumitra Chatterjee, Aparna Sen — people who represent a certain strand of liberal upper-middle-class culture with Tagore as its distant but distinguishable fountainhead. Perhaps in Ghatak, there is a nostalgic harking back to the days of IPTA when the avant-garde of the English-educated Bengali middle class went through its earlier wave of identification with the common people and tried to take its folk traditions into the modern world. The failure of that noble effort, its petering out in the 1950s, forms part of Ghatak's consciousness and gives a tragic colour, an almost revivalist shade, to his entire outlook. In Sen there is no such compulsive looking back ; the IPTA philosophy and its techniques are just a part of his background, as they are of so many others in Bengal. In fact, of the three, he is the most free not only from Bengali but Indian tradition as well. His search for identity is purely in terms of distinctiveness of style and statement. His entire evolution from *Raat-Bhor* to *Bhuban Shome* is dedicated to this search.

No wonder Ray is the rationalist among them. Except where he is formally engaged in fantasy as in *Goopi Gain Bagha Bain*, addressing himself mainly to children (or when he designs a disastrous dream-sequence as in *Nayak*), narrative logic is of the greatest importance to him. Besides, he is the conscious artist, and takes pride in knowing exactly what he is doing, impatient with suggestions of any meaning beyond or besides what he himself intended. Ghatak believed in the magical aspects of creativity and talked often of the Jungian unconscious and the universality of the mother cult. In an interview he clearly says that he often does not know what impelled him to make a certain sequence in a certain way and not another. Mrinal Sen's work is closely concerned with narrative logic in the same way as Satyajit Ray's ; but in the phase since *Akash-Kusum,* there is a constant interplay between naturalism and fantasy. In *Matira Manisha* and *Bhuban Shome* he shows a nonchalant, almost airy, disregard for narrative logic. And gets away with it.

Misconceptions about the high quality of Bengali cinema as a whole result from the reputation of these three directors. The bulk of Bengali cinema remains enveloped in sentimental verbiage uninformed by any understanding of the medium. Much of it is second-hand literature misprinted on celluloid, full of theatrical contrivance.

It would be natural to expect Satyajit Ray to have had a profound influence on Bengali, if not Indian, cinema as a whole. On retrospect, his direct influence seems to have been very little. Immediately after *Pather Panchali* the frontiers of the cinema did look wide. The success of his example inspired some thinking people to turn to the cinema. Some of those who had been hibernating within the film industry also felt encouraged to come out of hiding. But the euphoria did not last long. Many fell by the wayside or went back into hibernation within the conventions of the film industry. The old hands also learnt a few new tricks but changed little of their thinking.

In the wake of *Pather Panchali* came a spate of films which mistook the outward features of that film for the reason of its excellence. There was a rush for the great outdoors ; folk music, Indian classical music, invaded the screen ; heavy make-up and over-filtered photography beat a hasty retreat ; effect tracks became overloaded with train whistles and bird twitter ; dialogue was not to be found even where it was urgently required. The most complete example of this was in Rajen

Tarafdar's *Antariksha* which carried a whole *Pather Panchali* inside it like a baby kangaroo. Reels upon reels passed but nothing happened but a cat licking its paws or sunlight falling on a broken wall. There was immense relief when the first words were spoken and an experienced actor entered the scene. Tarafdar recovered from this rather splendidly in his next film, *Ganga*. He gave full play to his own inclinations, very much for the better. He brought off a few fine sequences, and despite his rather overblown romanticism, managed to convey a genuine feeling for his fisherfolk. With its against-the-light photography and shimmering reflectors, its surfeit of music worked rather better than his naturalism. The river is always a little too silvery, the clouds billowing and the girls hip-swaying a little too much. Nevertheless, it has some highly effective moments, such as the one in which the fisher-folk look for one of their men who has been devoured by a tiger. The film certainly commands one's attention, and the large mass of characters led by the first masculine hero of the Bengali cinema (curiously unheard of since), finally gives you a feeling of truth, perhaps because of the less decorative second half.

Films like Agragami group's *Dak Harkara* (1958) and *Headmaster* (1959) assayed sentimental subjects with a deter-mined devotion to poverty and nature photographed against-the-light understandably without getting anywhere. Debaki Bose, one of the oldest and most respected names in the Bengali cinema and creator of some of its landmarks like *Chandidas* (1932), made *Sagar Sangame* (1959) entirely outdoors without any of the trappings of commercial glamour. The result was not epoch-making, but a good clean film with a well-told story, which is more than what one can say for the products of younger men launching themselves in Ray's path of glory. Tapan Sinha at times spoke against neo-realism but tried his hand at it nonetheless in *Kshaniker Atithi*, producing a piece of naturalistic and actionless narrative with-out much significance but not without some charm.

Among film-makers in Bengal in this period, Sinha's case is the most curious. Basically grounded in conventional Ben-gali cinema and with little interest in the creative-technical

inventions which a personal statement demands, he has nevertheless fluctuated between the *Kabuliwala*-like conventional
picture-drama on celluloid and new directions as in *Kshaniker
Atithi, Nirjan Saikate* (1963), and *Atithi* (1965), without any
commitment to an outlook or a sense of intellectual-emotion-
al growth. He thus zigzags from *Kshaniker Atithi* (1959)
with its personal, naturalist-neorealist bias to the conventional-
dramatic formula of *Kshudita Pashan* (1960), making of the
Tagore story what any other director of average competence
would have done. From *Nirjan Saikate*'s distinctive comic
charm woven out of the lives of five widows finding solace in
togetherness, he turns to the didactic and unreal formula of
Aarohi (1964) and back again to a naturalistic 'flow-of-life'
film in *Atithi* (1965), then on to the unspeakable artificiality
and melodrama of *Sagina Mahato* (1969). No director works
in simplistic, continuous lines so as to make it convenient for
the critic to categorize him in felicitous phrases; but oscilla-
tions of Tapan Sinha's variety suggest the absence of any con-
tinuing concerns, either of form or content, even of serious
interest in the medium.

Interest in the medium is evident in the case of Asit Sen
(*Chalachal*, 1956, *Panchatapa*, 1957), a fine technician
who has learnt a lot from Hollywood. There are clever cinematic patches in his films; the remarkable use of a whistled
tune in *Deep Jele Jai* (1959), the giant machinery of emergent
India seen in new perspectives in *Panchatapa*, the vividly
realised surgical operation (a favourite subject of Bengali
directors, mostly poorly executed) in *Chalachal*. But his
content is abjectly conventional and the sum total never rises
above the commonplace.

Ajoy Kar, a more senior technician with a good deal of
polish, is in a similar position. Films like *Shuna Baranari*
(1960) are, in their own way, expertly scripted and cast, photographed and edited, and provide good clean 'entertainment'.
The use of trains in the image and sound track has nothing
original for those who see international films but is nevertheless admirable for its aptness. Here is a professional job,
done as a job and nothing else. The style of lighting and
photography continues to belong firmly to the 1930s, un-

touched by the winds blowing with the First International Film Festival, 1952.

What this means is not that there is no talent on the scene. In fact there are many talented directors, both of the traditional kind and others bearing the post-*Pather Panchali* stamp ; but what has prevented them from emerging into significant creativity has been a lack of deeper intellectual concerns and a sense of involvement with social problems around them. Talent has often been frittered away on insignificant subjects, superficial emotionalism without the adequate intellectual ability to give them any depth, resulting in contentment with minor creative inventions. The lack of anything to say has stultified many with the technical ability to say it. Among them one would name Partha Pratim Chowdhury whose *Chhayasurya* (1963) showed a good deal of promise but whose later work betrayed an unfortunate lack of maturity ; his mentor, Asit Sen, whose work has already been discussed; and Hari Sadhan Das Gupta, whose *Eki Ange Eto Roop* (1965) had all the marks of a fine craftsman but fell flat because of an inner void, both intellectual and emotional (some of his early documentaries like *Panchthupi* had shown more personal involvement with characters and situations). Rajen Tarafdar, who had shown a capacity for passionate involvement in *Ganga,* which has been already discussed, petered out into the commonplace in his later films. There was promise in the dreamlike quality of Purnendu Patrea's *Swapna Niye* (1960) — a fine visual sense and an emotional involvement with his subject, albeit one that overwhelms him.

In other words, apart from Satyajit Ray as also Ritwik Ghatak and Mrinal Sen, the Bengali cinema has been without any directors of notable individuality or sustained universal resonances in their work. The average product of the Bengali cinema continues to retreat before the superior technical gloss and uninhibited indulgence of the all-India film in Hindi into its regional heritage. In the process it has lost even the contemporary quality and the superiority of subject matter that the Bengali film used to enjoy. The future of the regional film as entertainment has been in doubt for some time all over India ; but nowhere more so than in West Bengal.

1966

are film societies necessary ?

In his book, *Documentary* : *A History of the Non-Fiction Film,* Eric Barnouw brings out the interesting connection that has almost always existed between the documentary film and the film society movement.

The Film Society, London, was founded in 1925, and within four years, premiered John Grierson's first film, *Drifters,* which was to herald the world's richest crop of documentaries at one time and in one country. The first French cine club was founded in 1924. The film-making that resulted from it was dominated by the painters; but in playing with the fragments of actuality, they had a strong documentary connection. In 1927, Walter Ruttmann's *Berlin : Symphony of a Great City* created enough impact to get a theatrical release. Jean Vigo was a leader of the Nice cine club and made, like Ruttmann and many others after him, a film on his city, *A Propos de Nice,* in 1929. At about the same time, Henri Storck founded a cine club in the Belgian seaside town of Ostende. In 1930 came his first film, again a city film, *Images d'Ostende.* Joris Ivens began by founding the cine club Filmliga in Amsterdam and in 1928 made *The Bridge,* about a railway bridge in Rotterdam. In Japan, the Proletarian Film League or Prokino was founded in 1929 and found an enthusiastic recruit in Fumio Kumei, who made a series of highly controversial films, many of them banned by Imperial Japan. The Film and Photo League was founded in the United States in 1930 and counted among its members Willard Van Dyke and Ralph Steiner, who made the short film *Hands* and generally unleashed a force that soon drew the towering talent of Pare Lorentz, maker of the famous documentaries, *The River* and *The Plow That Broke the Plains*.

These early film societies invariably represented a protest against the dream factories of commercial cinema, an urge for social concern, and in consequence a crusade for documentary realism. Speaking at the Films Division of the Government of India during a visit shortly before his death, John Grierson talked about Edgar Anstey's intense concern over the social problem of housing in contemporary Britain, and his absence of concern for awards for his art. This to Grierson, was what turned *Housing Problems* (1935) into a powerful work. In 1933, the Brussels cine club had financed Storck's film *Borinage* on the problems of coal miners; he made the film underground and was constantly shadowed by the secret police. The painters who crowded into the cine clubs of Paris in the middle twenties were impatient with the commercial cinema and wanted to show what the new medium could do. Their ranks included as hallowed a name as that of Fernand Léger, who made *Ballet mechanique*.

Invariably, the enthusiasm for starting a cine club was triggered off by the experience of seeing films which showed either the possibilities of the film medium outside its commercial-exploitative routines, or registered social protest effectively, usually both. Grierson's enthusiasm was fired by seeing Eisenstein's *Battleship Potemkin,* Storck was inspired to start the Ostende cine club after seeing Flaherty's *Moana* at the Brussels cine club; Boris Kaufman's collaboration with Jean Vigo on the latter's *A Propos de Nice* began as a result of seeing Dziga-Vertov's films when Vigo was the enthusiastic founder-leader of the Nice cine club.

Antagonism between the film society movement and the commercial cinema was so strong that Adrian Brunel, an employee of Gainsborough Pictures and a founder-member of the Film Society, London, was ordered by his employers to sever all connection with the society. Invariably, the film industry saw the film societies as discreditors of its own standards and as a threat to their hold on the audience. When Pare Lorentz's documentaries in the United States made a profound impact on the Depression audience and President

Roosevelt decided to promote such films governmentally, Hollywood marshalled the forces of private enterprise to demolish this intolerable piece of New Deal socialism—with complete success. Yet it was the Film Society, London, that activated the British documentary which, in turn, inspired the British feature film. Emotionalized by the tensions of war into stirring cinema for the first time in its history, its strength was in the understatement that came from the realistic language of the documentary.

Thus criticism of the mores of the commercial cinema has been an integral part of film society activity, reflecting the dissatisfaction of the intellectual, the artist, and the social reformer with the pedestrian and cynical exploitation of a medium of great artistic possibility and social power by entrepreneurs who put money before everything else. Film criticism has had a close link with the film society. Louis Delluc, pioneer of the cine club movement in France, was also a pioneer, alongside Leon Moussinac, of independent film criticism as opposed to publicity which masqueraded in its name. The French Federation of Film Societies has for many years published the highly rated journal *Cinéma*. *Sight & Sound*, British Film Institute's quarterly journal, relies heavily on the readership of the 700-odd member societies of the British Federation of Film Societies. A cyclostyled bulletin of the Film and Photo League of New York, *Film Front*, had a strong impact on a whole group of film-makers of the thirties. *Sequence*, edited successively by Gavin Lambert, Penelope Houston (both later editors of *Sight & Sound*), and Lindsay Anderson, was published by the Oxford Film Society, and had considerable influence on young film-makers, leading upto what became known as Free Cinema in the late fifties and early sixties. The Film Society of Lincoln Center, New York, publishes the well-known journal *Film Comment*, The British Federation of Film Societies publishes *Film*, the Swedish Federation, *Film Rutan*, and so on. All these journals share one common point of view; they are independent magazines of film criticism, far removed from 'publicity criticism'.

In most countries, film societies wrested the right to see

films in their uncensored form, and even films banned within the country.   Thus *Battleship Potemkin,* which was not allowed in the theatres in most places in the twenties and thirties was shown in film societies, notably the Film Society, London, which began this trend.   In Amsterdam the Filmliga's showings of foreign films included those not allowed to Dutch theatres.   The right of artists to view such films in privacy had been upheld after a stormy 1927 incident in which the police tried to stop a screening of Pudovkin's *Mother.*

It was the impulse generated by pioneer film societies which radiated towards the growth not only of independent film criticism and film-making but of art cinemas as well.   The first art cinema was opened in Paris by Armand Tailler in 1926.   His object was to provide exhibition opportunities for good films which were too limited in their appeal for the wide flung commercial cinema.   His inspiration caught on so well that by 1929 there were twelve such specialized cinemas in Paris (today their number is about fifty).   Leon Moussinac visualized an art cinema movement so strong that it would be able to commission and guarantee the distribution of films by talented directors otherwise ignored and suppressed by the film industry.   This is more or less what happened when Godard's *Breathless* was made for the equivalent of four lakhs of rupees in 1959; its cost was low enough, and film aficionados numerous enough to make it, and the early Nouvelle Vague, economically viable.   Film societies, art cinemas, books and journals had already nourished an informed minority audience of considerable proportions.

The first film society in India was founded in Bombay in 1937.   It was called Amateur Cine Society and had among its leading lights Rudy von Leyden, the art critic, and Dr Pati, the pioneer documentary film-maker trained in film-making in France, who later joined forces with Paul Zils.   The prime mover was Derek Jeffries who carried on its activities for a long time.   It was a small group of aficionados without much impact on the wider public or the film industry.   A similar group, the Bombay Film Society, started in 1942, again with the participation of documentary film-makers Clement Baptista, Vijaykar and commentator Samuel Berkeley Hill. Although both societies functioned for decades, they were too far ahead of their times and did not stimulate any writing or film-making capable of stirring up the stagnant waters of Indian cinema or standards of film appreciation.

The Calcutta Film Society was founded at a more propitious time, the year of Independence, by Satyajit Ray, myself and other enthusiasts. Among those who were to enrich Indian cinema with their talent were Subrata Mitra, a still photographer who was later to become one of the foremost cinematographers in the world and the cameraman of a series of films of Satyajit Ray. Nimai Ghosh, also a cameraman, later heralded the realism of *Pather Panchali* with his *Chhinnamool* (1953) shot in part on the platforms of Sealdah railway station bristling with refugees from East Pakistan. His collaborator in this was no less a person than Ritwik Ghatak, a frequenter of the society who turned into the venerated enfant terrible of the Bengali cinema. Hari Sadhan Das Gupta became one of the early recruits of the movement, immediately after his return from the film school of the University of California, Los Angeles, and went on to assist Jean Renoir in the making of *The River* (1949) and to make several notable documentaries of his own, such as *Panchthupi, Konaraka* (shot by Claude Renoir), *Weavers of Maindargi* and others.

Although it began as a small group and remained so till 1956, the society made a lot of noise. Poets and painters came to its shows; its discussion meetings generated heat; its outspoken criticism of the film industry attracted attention and counterattack. It exposed a small but vocal and influential audience to examples of world cinema which had not been seen before, and when seen, created instant impact. The society imported a copy of *Battleship Potemkin* and screened it several times. Jean Renoir addressed a meeting, and so did V. I. Pudovkin and Nikolai Cherkassov. The association with Renoir during his visits in 1948-49 first to reconnoitre and then to shoot his film, held up a model in film-making, and strengthened and broadened humanist ideas. Satyajit Ray wrote about him in *Sequence* and others, including myself, in local papers. Pudovkin showed his *Storm over Asia* and

7

narrated his experiences in filming it to a jampacked film studio. The society was the only group that honoured him as a film-maker rather than as a member of the Supreme Soviet; it was also the only body of people who knew anything about Renoir's work, and admired both as great film-makers to a somnolent, isolationist and self-satisfied film industry, duly incurring its wrath. It sent tickets to all members to see Uday Shankar's *Kalpana* and held an animated discussion afterwards. It published a bulletin from time to time. It was its members and supporters who banded together to bring out a substantial miscellany of serious film criticism in Bengali called *Chalachchitra* published by Signet Press, Calcutta, with contributions and editing by Satyajit Ray, Kamal Majumdar (who later made a considerable impression as a Bengali writer), R. P. Gupta, Subhas Sen and myself.

In 1952 came the first International Film Festival of India. At that time the society was the only body of people with some knowledge of international cinema, and it offered its advice which was accepted with alacrity by its organiser, J. N. Ganju. The festival made a profound impression on Calcutta's public and its would be film-makers. The encounter with Italian neorealism with its strong social concerns, coming after the exposure to Renoir's humanism, gave a sense of direction to the new aspirants; so much so that it proved to be a setback to the film society, whose slender activities in film viewing and discussion could not contain the spurt of creative energy generated by the festival. Satyajit Ray concentrated on the making of *Pather Panchali,* and others too began to think more about film-making than mere appreciation.

Chinnamool had already been made in 1953, and in 1955 came Ray's *Pather Panchali* which, after two weeks of hibernation in near-empty theatres, began to draw large audiences and went on to become a box-office hit. It was so unlike anything the Bengali cinema had seen before that a new force, associated with the film society movement and all that it stood for, had to be acknowledged suddenly by a very wide public. In 1956, Marie Seton gave a series of lectures at Indrapuri Studio (earlier the scene of Pudovkin's historic talk on the making of *Storm over Asia*) which stirred up a fresh interest in film appreciation along a wider front, resulting directly in the revival of the Calcutta Film Society on a larger scale. Within months of the inaugural (attended among others by Arne Sucksdorff), the membership climbed to several hundreds, and the film society movement in Bengal has never looked back.

The need to combine with like-minded groups on an all-India platform was soon felt and in December 1959 at the initiative of the Calcutta Film Society a meeting of seven society representatives took place at the house of Krishna Kripalani in New Delhi to form the Federation of Film Societies of India. The FFSI had its headquarters in Calcutta and branch offices in Delhi and Bombay. Satyajit Ray became president (and remains so) and Indira Gandhi, vice-president (remained so till 1967); Vijaya Mulay was joint secretary first in Delhi and then in Bombay, still later becoming vice-president; also active in Delhi were Usha Bhagat and I. K. Gujral (later to become Union Minister for Information and Broadcasting). The membership of the Federation climbed steadily, twenty coming into being in Bengal alone and several in metropolitan cities and state capitals. In Madras Shrimati Ammu Swaminathan was vice-president; in Bombay, Anandam and Film Forum (run by Basu Chatterjee, later a notable director) made great contributions, the first bringing out many publications climaxed by the Satyajit Ray number of *Montage,* the latter holding festivals of Prabhat Films, New Theatres, films of Ritwik Ghatak, Hemen Gupta, Mrinal Sen and others and publishing valuable booklets on these. Bengal came out with little magazines galore which died out as fast as they came, but a few continued publication over the years.

Meanwhile Calcutta Film Society made a city film, *Portrait of a City* (directed by me), which was nationally distributed by the Films Division in 1962 and resulted in the inclusion of the society in the roster of approved producers as well as in the making of two other films. Cine Central, another premier society in Calcutta, made a short film some years later. Chitralekha Film Society in Trivandrum formed a cooperative of filmmakers which has made feature film production possible for a number of new aspirants and has played an important part in the rise of a new cinema in Kerala. The FFSI started a magazine of its own, first called *Indian Film Quarterly,* then *Indian Film Review* and finally *Indian Film Culture.* Only some fifteen issues were published in all, but its influence was out of all proportion to its output. Film societies in many centres have run film appreciation courses and seminars, some in association with the Film and Television Institute and the Film Archives in Poona. In Bombay, the Drishti Film Society was formed solely to cultivate knowledge of the best of Indian cinema.

The FFSI succeeded in wresting from government that prime privilege of film societies all over the world — the right of students of the cinema to see films without the distortions of censorship. The Central government agreed that any film recommended by the FFSI president, Satyajit Ray, for the viewing by the member societies would be exempt from censorship. At the local level, most authorities agreed to exempt member societies of FFSI from entertainment tax. FFSI also came to terms with foreign missions — in the absence of organised import, still the largest suppliers of outstanding films to film societies — to route them through the FFSI which distributes them after determining their suitability. The National Film Archive of India began to lend some films from their collection. Naturally, film societies proliferated. By 1967, there were nearly a hundred.

But danger signals were also up. In 1967, at the All-India Conference of Film Societies, a debate came up on the advisability of indiscriminate growth of film clubs, many of them divorced from the objectives of the movement, and whether they should be granted membership. Socialist rhetoric won the day, and the call for cautious growth ensuring conformity to objectives of the Federation went unheeded.

By this time, it had become apparent that the privilege of seeing uncensored films was attracting a new type of membership which was not primarily interested in good cinema. Its numerical strength soon created pressures on film society secretaries which, they, perpetually short of funds, were hardly in a position to resist. This brought in its wake some amount of financial corruption (alleged misuse of and blackmarketing in admission cards) and not-so-cultural politics. Some societies, like the premier one of Anandam in Bombay, closed down; many underwent a change of character, becoming more like art theatres, showing good foreign films. Certain embassies dined, wined and cajoled film society leaders into showing any film they offered, without selection by the Federation. Discussions, publications, programme notes, libraries took the back seat with many and sometimes disappeared. Many a film society secretary was devoid of any film culture, and not far removed from cultural illiteracy.

Three other factors contributed to this situation: the absence of art theatres to show good films from all over the world to a wider audience; lack of imports from a wide variety of countries; and the strictness of censorship at a time when the permissive mores of industrial society had created a yawning gap with standards in India. The situation was further confused by the official film festivals which were, by international convention, exempted from censorship and yet thrown open to the widest possible public that used its black money and muscle power to corner tickets, elbowing out the intellectuals and the genuine enthusiasts of international cinema. The holiday from censorship celebrated by the annual international festival and the smaller but more frequent individual country festivals began to equate film societies with the mass audience that sat uncomprehendingly through Fellinis and Jancsós for that occasional glimpse of nudity denied to them in Indian cinema.

Had it been possible in the mid-sixties when the film society movement as a whole was at its peak of quality and well on the rails of its objectives, to make the government treat it as a major wing of film development like the Film and Television Institute or the Children's Film Society, the movement might have taken a different course. A greater sense of direction and a constructive development might have resulted had film society leaders made the policy but left financial and professional management to the government. This may still work out today.

Today, there are more than two hundred film societies within the Federation and hundreds are seeking admission. Unless a regular arrangement is made for importing films for film societies, it is not possible (nor, in the long term, desirable) for supplies from foreign embassies to fill the entire demand for good films from all over the world. In spite of their many shortcomings, and in spite of their functioning simply as art theatres, they still do provide a steady exposure to good international cinema round the year to some 100,000 people, not all of whom are in exclusive search of explicit sex scenes. A great many films, completely devoid of any prurient interest, are shown at film societies and large audiences attend the shows. Many societies, for instance, in Bengal, continue to publish little magazines of some significance. Film societies still represent the largest body of informed people capable of appreciating outstanding international cinema. First in Bengal, then notably in Kerala and Karnataka and Bombay, the film society movement has been involved with, and responsible for, the rise of a new, serious approach to cinema. To condemn the entire movement on account of a minority driven by prurient interest would be to throw out the baby with the bathwater. A change of bathwater can in fact improve the baby. The film society movement, already significant in this respect, can be made an important instrument of the large-scale spread of film appreciation, the growth of good film criticism, and thus provide the springboard for a better cinema.

1973

the golden age of Indian cinema: still to come?

The social conditions in which Indian cinema functions are utterly different from those of the West. As a mass medium the cinema in the West is on the decline. Unemployment and desolation stalk Hollywood, the mainspring of the mass cinema in the world for more than half a century. Cinema audiences have also slumped in Japan, which used to be at the top of the list of film-making countries. Film-making is more and more sharply polarized between the blockbuster and the 'personal' film. Serious cinema in the industrially advanced countries is fast becoming an aesthete's medium, addressed to an audience of the initiated. If it is not a *2001 Space Odyssey* in size and spectacle, its exposure area is in film societies, art theatres, student campuses. Its main direction of growth is towards the use of super-eight and other inexpensive ways which turn film-making into a do-it-yourself exercise for large minorities of people in industrially advanced, technically oriented countries — countries where gadgetry and audio-visual mechanics are a part of everyday life.

The number of people in France who are, or have been members of film clubs, attend shows at the cinema e or at one of the 50-odd art theatres in Paris, read seri film magazines and books, receive some education in film a cia-tion through universities and other agencies, was su tly large to support the film-making of Truffaut and Goda ven in 1959, when their first films surfaced. Such audien an recognise allusions to previous films or even clips fr ld newsreels and appreciate in-jokes about film personaliti It is doubtful if a comparable audience assembled in India would fill one cinema theatre for one whole week. The impact of television has turned avant-garde Western cinema away from the narrative realism which was the key to its mass contact and driven it towards a medium for the film buff. The change is in some ways comparable to the movement away from the figurative to the abstract brought about in painting by the impact of photography in the nineteenth century.

India today has about 300,000 television sets and within the next few years the figure may climb to a million; but the country's population is close to 600 million and the price of a television set is upwards of Rs. 3,000. With some 50 per cent of the people of the country below the breadline and a per capita income of less than Rs 600 a year at current prices, the prospects of television becoming a mass medium in India are remote.

The 300,000 television sets at present in operation are owned by the affluent minority and, for a long time to come, the pattern of television ownership is likely to remain the same. The cinema ticket is going to prove cheaper, even in the long run, than the television set perhaps for the next half century. What is more, the domination of the mass cinema over television is already apparent and is likely to increase. In radio the most popular programmes are the news broadcasts and film music. After a fruitless struggle All-India Radio had to give up its resistance to film songs. Already sports and film programmes are the mainstay of the popularity of television.

It seems likely that the cinema in India will continue to remain the most important mass medium for a long time to come and will dominate the medium of television. This has far-reaching implications for the orientation of the cinema in our country. It means that in India the medium can still attain the heights of a fusion between box office and art which was achieved in the past in other countries. The main difference between Hollywood at the height of glory and India producing some 440 films in 1973 lies in the absence of this fusion in our country. Within the severely limiting format of the box office, Hollywood produced Chaplin, Griffith, Erich von Stroheim, Josef von Sternberg, Ernest Lubitsch, John Ford, Alfred Hitchcock and innumerable others whose films made enormous amounts of money but are valid as cinema to this day. The Hollywood Western, the Hollywood musical, the Hollywood gangster film, the Hollywood comedy — all these genres threw up classic films in every period of Hollywood history. To this day major directors are making Western films for a mass audience and creating sufficient emotional and artistic satisfaction for themselves and their audiences. There are few film buffs in the world who would not like to see a Western such as William Wellman's *Yellow Sky* (1948) whenever there is an opportunity, or do not look forward to a revival of a musical like *Top Hat* (1935), a crime film like John Huston's *Asphalt Jungle* (1950) or Alfred Hitchcock's *Rear Window* (1953) or Chaplin's comedies dating from the First World War.

Why has this fusion not taken place in India ? Why is there almost no film which has made records at the box office and is also worth seeing today and is a piece of film art in the world context ? Why is it that Indian cinema for the masses has not made any contribution towards the development of film art in the world ? Why has it not invented new techniques, new equipment, which enrich this medium as a whole for its practitioners ? Why has it not added any really new expressions to the universal language of the cinema ? Why has Indian cinema had so little respect for itself that nobody bothered to save a copy of his film from oblivion so that posterity might see it ? Why are the unique features of Indian cinema essentially uncinematic, such as the picturization of songs; the very use of song and dance numbers in every kind of film interrupting the flow of the narrative ? Why does the mass film in India tend to become a variety performance ? Why is there no genuine division into genres like the Western or the crime film or the musical ?

To all these questions there is only one answer. The cinema is a product of industry. It is a technological medium created by technologically advanced countries. In the West, the people who make and the people who see them live in a technological environment and have done so for a long time. Three per cent of the population of the United States depends directly upon agriculture for a living, whereas in India 70 per cent of

the population does so.   In other words, in India, a technological medium has been superimposed on a non-technological
society.   That is why, in spite of its size and in spite of its
history being as long as that of Hollywood's, Indian cinema is
so far removed from the mainstream of world cinema developed in technologically advanced countries.   That is why
Indian cinema is closer in spirit and in technique to cinema in
Indonesia and Ceylon than to cinema in the United States or
the Soviet Union or France or, for that matter, Japan.   It is
only since Independence that technology has really begun to
develop in India, but, as is well known, the benefits of this
development have been cornered by the privileged classes, and
the masses of the people have gained very little from it.   The
country has grown richer but the people poorer.

Indian cinema of the period since Independence reflects this
reality.   Nehru realised the importance of the cinema immediately after Independence and in 1951 the Film Enquiry Committee made a comprehensive report on the state of Indian
cinema, which remains to this day the most authoritative
analysis of this subject.   In varying ways and to varying ex-
tents the recommendations of this commitee have been imple-
mented in the last quarter of this century, but the conditions
about which that report lamented have not improved.   The
artistic standards and the moral consciousness of the Indian
cinema, instead of improving, have deteriorated considerably
since then.   Vulgarity is no longer confined to an odd sequence
here and there; it is becoming the very stuff of the mass cinema.
It spreads itself from the very beginning of a film to its end.
The distortions of the urbanization process in India are clearly
reflected in the degeneration of the Indian mass films.   It is
becoming the cinema of the lumpen proletariat, the unemployed
half-educated or uneducated vagrant youth, the nouveau riche
with more money than education, the hoarder and the black
marketeer, the children and the adolescents born and brought
up on the pavements in large cities and living in the shadows
of high-rise buildings.

It is in this context that the phenomenon of the parallel
cinema in India must be viewed.   It is the product of the
government's efforts to improve the cinema.   It is symbolic

of the absence of effort to improve the mass cinema. It shows that the affluent minority of India whose size is that of a European country like Sweden has grabbed the benefits of development in this area as in all the others. The privileged class is in the process of creating entertainment for itself, leaving the masses to the mercy of their exploiters. While much of it is concerned with poverty and superstition, it is unable to communicate with the mass of the people affected by them.

The new cinema in India had started with Satyajit Ray but many of its new protagonists have left his social concerns by the wayside. Even when our new cinema deals with the rural setting, it often does so from the outside, in a decorative way, without identification with the common man. The greatest social reality of India is the poverty of the masses. The Indian film-maker who is able to forget this reality lives in an ivory tower which can be built only with black money. The Indian elite is less fearful about poverty itself than about what the foreigner says about it. Whenever a film showing the truth about the common man is shown abroad, our embassies get busy trying to prove that it is all either a matter of the past or a figment of the film-maker's imagination. The Indian elite lives under the compulsion of proving that it is as good as the elite in the West. This is why there is a compulsion also in the cinema to leave aside major social concerns in order to prove that we have our own Antonionis and Bressons. This is why so many of the films of this parallel cinema, Indian imitations, are so full of pretensions and aestheticism, spawned in the pavement cafés of Paris and the pubs of London. We forget that Antonioni or Bresson, Wajda or Makavajev, Godard or Truffaut, Tarkovsky or Ozu or Oshima have always been concerned with the major moral and social issues of their environment, and their techniques have grown organically from within their own context. They have spoken in a language that would be understood in their own society.

Technology has finally begun to grow all over India and is asking for fundamental changes in outlook on the part of the entire people. In the present context, our cinema, which will keep growing for a long time to come, is the best placed medium to provide a cultural leadership in bringing about the changes.   In other words, the popular cinema in India today is in need of a massive cultural input.   If that can be provided, the need for a parallel cinema kept alive by governmental oxygen will disappear.   The parallel cinema will then become the popular cinema's experimental laboratory for new ideas and techniques.

Indian cinema is yet to enter its golden age, its Shakespearean period, its Chaplinesque phase.   This will be a phase which, if I am allowed an idealised vision, will achieve a fusion of art and the box office in the best traditions of mass cinema in spite of box office constraints.   Its tasks will be to interpret the modern world to the common man, to discuss with him the shape of things to come, to create for him the   synthesis of age-old beliefs and the new ways brought about by science.

It will provide a cultural leadership to the masses.   It will not preach.   It will not try to 'educate'!   Its value to the masses will be similar to the value of the best of literature to the educated people.   Like literature, it will try to examine and understand all facets of life and create a culture out of that process itself.   Within its fold there will be religion, and there will be sex and violence, there will be spectacle, there will be song and dance, but all of it will have a valid artistic form, a valid spiritual relationship to tradition and in the modern world.

There will also be a kind of vulgarity in it — the smell of sweating bodies in jampacked theatres, the sound of monkey-nuts being cracked or loud yawns of boredom, of things being thrown at the screen with disapproval, of whistles rending the air at the sight of swaying hips in tight clothes.   Yet, its mental level will be such that the intellectual and the man in the street will not be ashamed to share its delights — at least until television does to us what it has done to cinema in the West; so India has still a chance to make it.

The Golden Age of the cinema was best expressed by the Hollywood Stuntmen Association's citation at the funeral of John Ford: 'one of us, and among the best'.

1975

Speaking in General

what is a good film?

Perforce, the title of this essay is a little silly. Nobody asks the question: What is a good book, or what is good music? It just seems unnecessary. But when it comes to the cinema, it rears its ugly head not because it is a new medium but because the cinema appears to be a colossal dream-factory whose products are marketed through the highly commercial channels of a worldwide entertainment industry, riddled with blackmarketing in tickets, torn posters of nearly topless female torsos displayed on urinal walls, mile-long queues of truant school boys and urchins with unruly hair and a rolling gait, entertainment tax, fire-prevention laws, censorship acts and an endless row of other things which make its whole look and feel seem utterly different from the esoteric world of books and music.

Pop music and paperbacks displaying females with improbable bosoms represent no less a threat to classical music and serious writing than the entertainment whirligig of the cinema does to the film as an art. There are many kinds of books and many kinds of music. There are also many kinds of films.

Yet films, no matter how full of high art, must be made and shown through modern industrial-commercial means; writing and music may also be, but need not. The director of the most contemplative, inward film cannot merely be a creative artist; he must, at the same time, be something of a manager of a factory. Films must be shot through highly sophisticated machines, on chemically sensitized lengths of celluloid; developed and printed in elaborate chemical laboratories; recorded through precision products of sound engineering, edited on moviolas, and projected to the audience though equally complicated sound projectors with high intensity arcs burning carbons. All this equipment is itself mass produced by major engineering and chemical industries employing large numbers of people and requiring high degrees of skill. A film-making crew is like the set-up of a factory — managers, technicians, workers all functioning under the director of the film. All this belongs to the world of finance, commerce and technology. Standing in the middle of it all is the director who wishes to express himself like an author or a composer and who must be a creative artist. It is as if the contradiction between ends and means is complete. Yet from this contradiction Griffith, Chaplin, Eisenstein, Renoir, Dreyer — to name only a few — extracted powerful works of literature or music. Today Bergman, Fellini, Antonioni, Kurosawa, Ford, Truffaut and our own Satyajit Ray carry on the tradition of deep emotional expression through complex technology. It is for this reason that the cinema, of all arts, is the closest to the spirit of our times.

Like all languages, the language of the cinema too must be learnt. It has developed its own particular conventions, styles of phrasing which the audience gets so used to that if only a part of it is indicated, the rest is readily understood. The connotation of words changes from age to age often in defiance of the dictionary, getting richer in the process, and able to evoke great ranges of associated images and feelings. When the close-up was first used in the cinema, the audience shrieked, horrified by the sight of the dismembered head. The movement of a character from one place to another had to be shown in great detail, so that the audience did not lose the thread of it. When Orson Welles in *Citizen Kane* recorded a continuous conversation between two characters and showed them in different situations and different costumes at the same time, the audience found it difficult to follow his train of thought. Today close-ups cause no surprise, and the audience is not disturbed to see a character now in one place and the next moment in another. Our enjoyment of the epics or of Shakespeare today stands greatly enriched by all that has been written and said about them for ages. Even in the young art of the cinema a good deal has been written and said which leads to a greater understanding of the medium and helps us to answer the question: What is a good film?

But one must begin at the point where all art begins. All art must synthesize the chaotic world of human experience and meaningfully communicate the artist's thoughts, feelings, emotions, attitudes arising from the process back to that world. But the camera is a machine which faithfully records physical reality. In the early days of the movies, excitement was produced by the mere fact of seeing rushing waves, passing trains, racing horses. Even today most films impress their audience by their scale and skill of representation — an army of extras in imperial Rome; a bevy of beautiful girls on the beach; a vast landscape with galloping horses on 70-mm screen caught in vivid colours; a novel or a play 'brought to the screen' with its attendant thrills of recognising known characters and speeches. Skill is mistaken for art. The artist is an individual. No matter how corporate the means of art may be, the final product must be the expression of an individual mind. The complex technology and the corporate skill that go into film-making tend to obscure the role of the individual mind that creates the whole. Indeed the attempt in the entertainment film industry is to kill it as far as possible. Selznick castigated King Vidor for calling the movies an art; and the best of the Hollywood artists — like John Ford — hotly denied that they were doing anything but making money for their studios.

Imitation, representation, recording, reconstruction, adaptation — these come easily to the cinema. What does not come as easily is the expression of the subjective feelings of the individual artist, the expression of his abstract ideas, the manifestation of the 'non-physical' through the physical. In judging the cinema, we must distinguish skill from art, representation from expression, and the individuality of the artist from the anonymity of imitation of outward reality. The measure of the goodness of a film, in other words, is not only in its skill to show us the physical reality, but the power of expression of the non-physical.

To the camera, a horse is a horse. In painting it can be distorted to express the artist's particular sense of form. As

8

Siegfried Kracauer points out, the camera photographs the
skin; it cannot, like an X-ray machine, show us what is under-
neath. Whatever it expresses must be through physical terms.
This has led some people to believe that the film is nothing
more than a documentary recording of reality, unable to express soul states like literature, or music, of which these other
media are capable. But because the cinema can bring to us
immediate experience of physical reality more completely than
any other art, it can also evoke in us the ambiguous, rich, many-
levelled reactions which we bring to bear on life itself. In
real life the sight of a horse can give us sensations of poetry,
of fear, of fascination with form, of sheer physical sense of
well-being according to the space-time context in which we
see it, its surroundings, and the events and emotions which
precede our act of seeing it.

This space-time context can be changed, selected and organised by the film director in such a manner as to evoke the
particular responses which he seeks in us at a time. And
because he has, unlike us, complete and continuous control over
what we see, and hear, the reactions he evokes are not fortuitous
and erratic as in real life, but capable of visualization in
advance. He not only selects what we see, but can emphasize
details which we may not have seen in real life and can place
them in any of an almost infinite number of permutations and
combinations of points of view, distance, length of time, inci-
dental sound, dialogue, imposing upon the whole a rhythm of
movement which appears to belong to reality but is in fact
created by him. He can add to it what may be an entirely
subjective dimension — background music — which does not
exist in real life. In other words, he can create the 'objective
correlative' of ideas, feelings, emotions and attitudes through
the selection and arrangement of fragments of reality and
turn them into a complete whole which represents a synthesis
of outward experience in order to create an inward reality.
Cartier-Bresson seeks the 'decisive moment' in his still photography — in a certain light, at a particular moment a face or a
landscape may express something which it does not at the
next moment, in a different light, in a different context. The
artist in the cinema can create a continuous flow of decisive

moments at which the visual object is at its most expressive and evocative condition.

Classical theories of the cinema usually discuss film purely in terms of the image. Undoubtedly the image is the basis; films can be made without sound, but not without images. But today's film form enriches its visual base enormously with words, natural sounds, and music — the first two of this add to the sense of immediacy which evokes the real-life responses in us in their most complicated form, inexpressible in any other medium, and the last adds a powerful instrument of direct 'subjectivization'.

Let us first take the example of dialogue. David Lean's *Brief Encounter* begins and ends in a restaurant at the railway station. The lovers are meeting for the last time. The train is about to arrive. Every minute is precious. They do not touch each other; they hardly speak, waiting for the horrible moment of final parting. Suddenly a portly, talkative woman, an acquaintance of the girl, sails in and starts an animated, entirely one-sided conversation about nothing in particular. They were ostensibly having a cup of tea and they offer her one. The man silently gets up and brings it, puts it down before her as she jabbers on. They cannot even look at each other, except incidentally, as it were. 'Where is the sugar, dear?' asks the garrulous woman. The man replies : 'It's in the spoon.' He looks at the girl. The train is announced, it is time to go. He takes leave of the garrulous one, puts a hand on his girl's shoulder, goes out. The girl continues to stare vacantly at her neighbour, who is still talking. On the stage or in the printed word, the dialogue quoted would sound ludicrously flat. But in the cinema, where the actors work within the full context, and extract meaning out of every detail, it immediately conveys a great deal, as in real life. Michael Rohmer says : 'All of us bring to every situation, whether it be a business meeting or a love affair, a social and psychological awareness which helps us to understand complex motivations and relationship.' This kind of perception, much of it non-verbal and based on apparently insignificant clues, is not limited to the educated or the gifted.

We all depend on it for our understanding of other people and have become extremely proficient in the interpretation of subtle signs — a shading in the voice, an averted glance. This nuanced awareness, however, is not easily called upon by the arts, for it is predicated upon a far more immediate and total experience than can be provided by literature and the theatre with their dependence on the word or by the visual arts with their dependence on the image — only film renders experience with enough immediacy and totality to call into play the perpetual processes we employ in life itself.

The silent cinema, working on only the visual aspect of experience, did not offer the same sense of complete immediacy, and did not call real life process into play to the same extent. It compensated amply for it by heightening the visual, by emphasizing relationships through montage, by giving everything a grand, heroic, generalized and symbolic character. *Battleship Potemkin* deals with contemporary reality and lifts it to heroic proportions; it gives a magnificent objective impression of the revolutionary impulse and conveys the combined feelings of a mass of people; but like all great silent cinema, it does not seek to portray the mind of the individual in a realistic, intimate manner. In *The Passion of Joan of Arc,* Dreyer draws upon four distinct elements: the fascinating expressiveness of the human face in close-up, the hypnotic and concentrative effect of rhythm of movement of object and camera, the arresting quality of strong formal compositions in black and white, and the revealing power of detail. When Joan looks to the priest for help, he averts his eyes. It has an iconographic quality of image, and the stylization helps the sense of remoteness in time. In *Ivan the Terrible* Eisenstein fused the main elements of almost all the other arts, but stylized them all, and in a way it was an extension of the stylization of the image sought by the silent film where the image was the sole aspect of reality presented and the director had to come forward to meet his audience halfway with clearly underlined relationship between the images.

In *Potemkin* the three famous shots of the sculptured lion

on the gate of the royal navy's headquarters produce the illusion of a lion rising to express an abstract idea, a literary metaphor. Many of Ivan's statements on the other hand are made directly in words and avoid the over-emphasis which a literary metaphor acquires in a purely visual medium. The coronation scene brings together the virtues of stylization in both silent and sound media. The historic nature of the event is brought out through the singing in rich bass tones as much as in the visual, showing a shaft of light falling on the young prince. The stylization suits the historical subject, and although working in sound, Eisenstein in effect extends his grand manner of silent cinema into it. What he would have done with an intimate contemporary subject in the sound period is anybody's guess.

Modern French film directors have extended the place for words in the cinema and in many ways not only modified but reversed the classical theories. In Resnais' *Last Year at Marienbad* or *Hiroshima mon amour* there is an almost total reversal of the concept of the cinema as a purely visual medium in which sounds, particularly words, are tolerated as an aid. Parts of *Hiroshima* have completely disconnected images which cannot be understood at all without the help of the words. *Marienbad* is almost completely a series of illustrations of a poetic commentary. While both may be symptoms of revolt against the establishment to put new life into the cinema, and the permanent mark they leave on the art may be far less revolutionary, the fact is that both give us a sense of exciting new frontiers of the cinema, extending its power of expressing ambiguity, subjectivity and musical evocation. In other words, the cinema's ability to express the non-physical through the physical is tremendously enhanced by the addition of sound, particularly words, and we must no longer think of it as a purely or even essentially visual medium but as a new compound of all the previous arts, visual and non-visual.

In our judgement of the cinema, therefore, we must look for sets of values. One is composed of cinematic values, the other, the values common to all arts. Cinematically, we look for the qualities which overcome the physical basis of the cinema and express the human mind, and the extent of utilization of the resources peculiar to the film medium. On the broader plane, we look for the individuality of the artist, the impact of his work and its memorability, the significance of what he has to say, the effect of time on his art — does it gain or lose its value as time goes on ? We consider his relationship with his society and his times and how much of this is expressed in his work. We reflect on his ability to excite us and disturb us on repeated examination, and make all the other tests we apply to works of literature or music in terms of form or content. Three silent films, all made in 1925, spring to mind — Chaplin's *Gold Rush,* Dupont's *Variety,* and of course, Eisenstein's *Battleship Potemkin.* Older techniques and costumes by themselves are what generally put us off — many people laugh when they see films of an earlier period. But as films like these unfold, they somehow make us forget that they were made decades ago, and envelop us in their own logic. It is a little like what happens in Indian classical dance and music. A performer like Ustad Nissar Hussain Khan (senior) would hold us in thrall with his *tarana* despite his pronounced lack of a melodious, 'true' voice, or Birju Maharaj make us forget his short stocky body within minutes of starting to do a *paran.* Seeing many of the film classics today is to discover new virtues in them. They are so compressed and have so many resonances and layers of meaning to them that it takes repeated viewings to get the full measure of their worth. Their images often have a power and inevitability of organisation which make them autonomous, memorable. It is as if they are not reflections of reality held before the camera, but independent images existing on their own. The close-ups of Dreyer's *Joan,* the steps of *Potemkin,* the mountain hut teetering on the brink of a precipice in *Gold Rush* all have this autonomy and memorability which is the hallmark of classic cinema.

As in all other arts, a characteristic of good cinema must also be the way in which it gets to the essence of the medium. The camera's freedom to see from far and near, above and below, in movement or in statis, gives the cinema a plasticity which only the best of its practitioners know how to use. Since what we see is a two-dimensional image, its sense of reality has to be reinforced through this plastic use of medium. Seeing it from different angles and movements gives the image its third dimension. That is why the stagey eye-level vision with horizontal exits and entrees, with characters lined up close to the background facing or presenting a profile to the camera is unbearable and ruins the good storytelling of so many regional films in India and the bulk of the commercial all-India film. The best in any medium brings us something that belongs completely to it and seems impossible to achieve in any other. The precise appeal of *Charulata* or *Rashomon* is all its own, not dependent on our awareness of the literary work of Rabindranath Tagore or Ryunosuke Akutagawa which inspired it. In spite of its deliberate theatricality and its static camera compositions, *Ivan the Terrible* is possible only in the cinema; even when Ozu uses the (Japanese) eye-level camera without movement, he does so in deliberate opposition to movement possibilities, using the static as means of creating a tension whose point of reference is the cinema's plasticity.

Traditionally, film criticism has divided films into two categories: those that spoonfeed instant entertainment to a passive audience, and those that excite the audience's imagination and make it participate in the experience The former has often been traced to the Lumière brothers who first made and showed films all over the world but believed the cinema was just a nine-day wonder and made money by startling audiences with trains and waves rushing at them. The other strand is of Georges Méliès, the magician, a contemporary of the Lumières, whose *Voyage to the Moon* still reverberates with his own inventive imagination and excites that of his audience. The DeMilles of the cinema are descendants of the Lumières, the artists of Méliès. Simplistic as this view may be, it does express the essential difference between film as ephemeral entertainment and as more enduring art. The manner in which a film is released today and disappears tomorrow brings pressure on it to make money here and now, and obscures any enduring late-flowering aspects the work may have.

The movie moghuls are impatient with films that may be understood and even imitated decades later, such as Jean Renoir's *La Règle du jeu* ('Rules of the Game') or Orson

Welles' *Citizen Kane,* both of which bewildered people at the time but became treasure houses for film-makers to hunt for creative invention in later times. This does not reduce the value of the time dimension in the cinema as an art; but because its industrial apparatus demands instant entertainment for a passive audience, many of its creative minds have had to cast their work in the Shakespearean mould to please both those that stay put and say, 'Entertain me !' and the others who come forward to meet the artist halfway, to participate and fill in the gaps he must leave for the active imagination with which he longs to communicate. Chaplin worked at many levels, the immediate and the enduring and complex; so did workhorses like John Ford who made the least prestigious films of Hollywood — the Westerns — and shied away, always, from the word 'art'. Shooting in his favourite valley, Ford instructed the first actor to cry 'Haalt' to the oncoming Indians, and the second actor to repeat the command, but 'only after the echo dies'. As the camera was about to roll, he repeated: 'Pat, remember, after echo dies.' Obviously he wanted the audience to hear that echo and to feel the texture of the sound.

Because the cinema commands such a power over large numbers of people, the businessman has sought to use it as entertainment to make money, the politician to perpetuate his rule, the missionary to propagate his zeal; few have loved it for its own sake, and all have been suspicious of the artist whose skill is essential to their design but whose art is an unwanted commodity. Caught among these ghouls of capitalism, socialism and moralism, the artist in the cinema lives a precarious existence; he fulfils himself only by cheating his master — slipping in what he wants beneath what the master decrees. Stroheim was caught doing this in Hollywood and Eisenstein in Russia, and both had to pay for their sins.

Even the so-called educated audience extorts a price from the artist in the cinema. Brought up on literary values, it wants a journalistic statement of ideas from Antonioni, demands political posture-mongering from Satyajit Ray, asking him to provide so-called positive solutions. It insists on strict adherence to literary sources for cinematic work. It keeps confusing the artist's subject-matter with his statement. They will not allow a film-maker to examine a subject without equating him with it; almost like the politician to whom a film on crime is itself criminal. The politician, besides, is suspicious of independent thinking, and totalitarianism puts mediocrity — safe and controllable — on a pedestal. To respond to the statement, literary or 'musical' in nature, that the director makes behind the appearance of his subject requires a participation which most audiences, even the 'educated', are often not prepared to grant him. Yet the difference between the cinema as ephemera and as art must remain predicated on this participation and determine, more than anything else, the answer to the question: What is a good film?

1965

the story
and the film

People love to see films of books that they have read — particularly well-known books. When *Hamlet* or *Othello* is shown, all the students and professors flock to see it. They are usually disappointed. They have been disappointed many times; yet whenever a film made from a famous book comes along, they flock to it again. They are disappointed because they go to see the book, and not the film. They are like doting fathers — or mothers — who are delighted to see a perfectly ordinary photograph of their son, even when the son is sitting right in front of them. A more expressive photograph of the child often disappoints them because the likeness may not be absolute. In fact, in Bengal, people actually use the word 'book' in place of the word 'film'. 'Have you seen Tapan Sinha's latest book ?' they will ask you, meaning his film, of course.

Unfortunately, people who make films often think in the same way, even if they do not use the word 'book' in place of the word 'film'. So in fact do a lot of people who think, talk and write about what's wrong with Indian films. Invariably they say, 'the trouble is our film people don't take good stories'. They make the same mistake as the average Bengali, only instead of using the word 'film', they use the word 'story'. They think the two are one and the same thing. If you press the question they will admit that a good film needs good camera work and sound, and even good direction. But basically, to them, the film is the story.

Let us assume for the moment that what these worthy gentlemen say is true. Let us suppose that five film directors accidentally make five films on the same story at the same time, suppose the story is of the battle of Kurukshetra. Let us say that you have the misfortune of seeing all of them. What will you find ? You will find that one film bores you to death; another is moving and exciting, beautiful; the third is good in patches, but on the whole so-so. In other words, you will find that the film is what the film director has made of it. A famous French film director once said : 'If I were the dictator of the film industry, I would force every director to make a film about the same story. From the results I would see who were the true artists and who were not. I would then stop the non-artists from making films. Imagine what that would do for the film industry.'

The moral of this story is that films are created the same way that other things are created. Tolstoy had a great story in *War and Peace*, the story of Napoleon's invasion of Russia. But would you say that *War and Peace* is a great novel because Napoleon invaded Russia) ? It is a great novel because it was written by a man who had a tremendous sweep of imagination, of feeling for history and for people, and a magnificent power of expression. The Hollywood film called *War and Peace* follows Tolstoy's novel, but what does it make of it ? It makes of Tolstoy's novel what Marie Corelli would have made of it if she had re-written Tolstoy. A petty director would have turned a fine novel like *Pather Panchali* into sentimental trash. In fact I doubt if anyone at that time would have filmed it at all, for it has hardly a story. It is just the story of life.

Why do people go to see films? Because they want to see other people. Through the experience of other people, they have a sense of experience. They go to see not what happens, but how it happens. After all, what can happen is limited. There is only a certain number of basic plots available in the world. There are endless repetitions of these same stories all over the world in literature and in films. People like seeing films about stories they know. Even when they don't know, they can more or less guess what is going to happen — except in some crime films. In other words, we go to see not events, but people. We want to live; that is why we are interested in others' lives, to see how they live, what they do. The endless variety of human nature and human relationships keeps our interest alive. No two human beings are exactly alike. Every face, every character, has something in common with others, and yet is different. It is this difference that makes us want to see other people, it never ceases to surprise us. We never stop wondering at this diversity. People's faces, their gestures, reactions, relationships, their love and hate, laughter and sorrow, hope and despair produce endlessly different combinations which go on surprising us. The film we see may be a fantasy. It may be a heroic spectacle which is longer than life; it may be everyday experience; but basically it is about life. The moment it looks real and true to us, we become interested.

It is this stuff of life that all true artists try to capture in their work. The film director does so as much as the novelist or the poet, the painter or the sculptor. He too must express his feeling for life through a form — the film. But he cannot express himself like the painter by taking up a brush or as the poet by taking up a pen. He has lots of hurdles to cross. He needs a man with some money; he needs a cameraman, a group of actors, and an art director, a sound recordist, a music director, a whole lot of assistants, and a vast number of machines of all kinds.

Physically, film-making is a group activity. But as creative work, it must be the product of an individual imagination. The first problem about the film form is that the business of its production is so complex, and has to go through so many processes. At any stage something can go wrong. It is through a constant struggle with obstacles that a fine film is created. The creative film director has a sort of vision of his film — he can see it, at least most of it, in his mind's eye. But having an image in your mind and putting it on film are two different things. Between the two lies a vast gulf which he has somehow to bridge in order to capture the image on a few thousand feet of celluloid and communicate to you what he feels and what he has to say. Of course, unless he has something to say, the whole process is a waste of time. And having something to say is not just having a good subject or story. It is something that is inside you — an outlook, emotions, feelings, sensations and thoughts which are communicated by the film director to his audience. It is not the eye behind the camera, but the mind behind the eye behind the camera that counts. But the mind must express itself through form. All poets have sung about love saying more or less the same things. It is only through the manner of expression, the images, the rhythm, the original use of words that we know the truth of one poem and the pretentious falseness of another. In film, too, the truth or falseness of the content becomes manifest in the form. The more true it becomes, the more it captures the essence of the form.

Throughout the long, complex, and troublesome process of film-making, the director must sustain, protect, and carry his vision in a pure uncontaminated state. It is like running a race on an uneven track with a spoonful of water in your hand. You must get there fast without spilling a drop. Look at the films which have come to be called the great films of the world — they all have the stamp of the individual genius on them. The *Gold Rush* is the essence of Charlie Chaplin; *Battleship Potemkin* is Eisenstein; *Bicycle Thieves* is Vittorio De Sica; *Rashomon* is Akira Kurosawa; *Pather Panchali* is Satyajit Ray.

The film form is made of images and sounds. An image is not merely a pictorial record, it should not be merely pretty like a picture postcard; it must be expressive, it must evoke feeling. A beautiful, evocative image often becomes memorable. That is why long after you have forgotten the story or a film you may remember some of its images — a girl combing her hair, a boy running across a field. Girls often comb their hair, and boys often run across fields. But only rarely does this action become a fascinating image. In a film which reaches the level of art, an image of ordinary things often becomes as memorable as a beautiful painting. Take, for instance, the image of the house skating about on the ice in Chaplin's *Gold Rush*. Or the perambulator rolling down the steps of Odessa in Eisenstein's *Battleship Potemkin*. Or the bandit walking through the forest, the blade of his axe catching the sun in Akira Kurosawa's *Rashomon*. Or the knight playing chess with death at the seashore in *Seventh Seal.* Or Apu and Durga leaning against the telegraph pole, listening to the sound of the wind against it in *Pather Panchali.*

To the sensitive film-maker sounds also have their beauty and meaning and help to make the image impressive — a dog barking in the middle of the night; a street vendor's voice on a Sunday afternoon; the clop-clop of a horse-drawn carriage; the sound of water dripping from a tap in the next room. Image and sound blend together in a plastic movement. From a vast landscape you suddenly change to a big close-up of a face. You can see the beads of perspiration forming slowly on it. Sometimes you are looking from above, sometimes from below. A horse is running forward towards you; a girl is walking away to the distance through an avenue of trees. Sound, too, recedes or comes forward, is loud as canons, or soft as footfalls. From scene to scene, the movement of sound and image can be fast as a race, slow as billowing clouds.

The film medium offers a tremendous range of plasticity. This, far from making the job easy, makes things more difficult. Where are you to start ? Where are you to place the camera ? What sound effect are you to use with this or that scene ? What kind of light should you have ? Anything will do as far as getting a scene on film is concerned. But anything will not do to make an exciting and beautiful film. The film must have a unity, not only of action, time and place, but of mood and atmosphere, camera technique, and above all, a unity of style. And the style of film-making comes entirely from the film director. He makes his mark through the originality of his vision, the unique quality of the images and sounds he creates, and the rhythm of their movement. His material may be a well-known book; but he is making a film not photographing a book. Take David Lean's *Great Expectations.* It brings Dickens to life as it were; but it succeeds in doing so only because the style of film-making is so fine, so sensitive. There is a true feeling for people and places; and that feeling comes, not from Dickens, but from David Lean.

There are many reasons why David Lean, or any other creative film-maker, goes to a good novelist for material. A known story has its advantages; its acceptance by the public is assured. But the more important reason is that a story gives us an organised succession of events and a great story often has an evocative power which becomes an inspiration and a starting point for the film director. After all, when you come to think of it, any man's life is a story, including yours and mine. Only no one has written it.

It is not easy to write a story. Where the film-maker finds a story in which the incidents and the lives of the people have already been organised for him, he feels justified in using it as a starting point. Many classic films have been made straight from film scripts, and not from books : most of the films of Eisenstein's, for instance. Or Chaplin's. Classic films have been made from famous stories; some of the world's worst films have also been made from very good stories. The fact thus remains — to the disappointment of many film reformists — that the story is not the film. Between the story and the film form stands the film director, who makes all the difference.

1964

↬ the screenplay
as literature

Afilm is primarily something to see, not to read about. No
description of a film can take the place of seeing it. Except
to the cinéaste, long descriptions of film sequences are more
than boring; they are strenuous, because they force us to conjure up the visual images and sounds in our minds. Seeing
is a simpler, more passive activity to most people than reading.
When the average film-goer settles down in the seat in the
cinema, he says to the screen : 'Come, entertain me ! I have
paid for it.'

Yet in the nearly eighty years of the cinema (how it creeps
on towards a century. It seems only the other day that we
used to talk of 'half-a-century of the cinema'), a considerable
amount has been written about it. Even descriptions, for one
of the commonest forms of film literature today is the scenario,
published in a readable form, like plays. With the increasing
recognition of the film as an art and the sophistication of its
forms, its audience has also widened from the 'Nickelodeon'
days to take in the most cultivated minds used to the mental
exercise of imagining the sights and sounds of film from the
written word. Literature has already demanded this ability
of us for a long time; novels have always abounded in long
passages of visual and aural evocation not very different from
film scripts.

Film societies, festivals, arthouses, institutes, books and journals on the cinema have given rise to a film culture among the
sophisticated — in the West anyway — which makes it still
easier for them to enjoy reading scenarios. And the great
film-makers whose films and filmscripts are worth the study,

have, almost without exception, been men of high general culture, able to express themselves forcefully through the written word. Chaplin, once the idol of the mass audience, is one of the most cultivated clowns the world has ever produced. Ingmar Bergman has been a famous director of plays; Jean Cocteau had been a noted designer, poet, and painter; Jean Renoir has written a fine biography of his father, and his latest novel, *Les Cahiers du Capitaine Georges* (now translated into other languages), has been considered remarkable in France. Eisenstein was a genius of a teacher and writer who drew upon the history of diverse cultures of the word in his lectures and essays to produce some of the best theoretical writing of our times. Indeed this is inevitable to the cinema because it demands a complex understanding of all the previous arts from which it distils its own. Its dimensions of image, natural sounds, music, words and their infinite combinations reach out into the history and texture of painting, sculpture, architecture, music, drama and literature to fashion them into an art for this age of science.

The orchestration of all these diverse elements requires the word-symbol as much as a symphony requires its notation. But words, unlike notations, can have a life of their own, and a scenario can become literature when it is the product of a creative talent. Eisenstein's script for *Que Viva Mexico* has become one of the classics of film literature. His treatment for Theodore Dreiser's *An American Tragedy* is an even better example, because it was never made into a film. To those whose sensibilities have been trained in the language of the cinema, its evocation is perfect. The enjoyment of such a screenplay has itself become an important sign of the interaction of the arts within the wide range of the cultivated mind in our time.

The surface of Big Bittern lake.
Pools of the inky black surface of the silent water.
Their gunwales against a rude landing stage at the footsteps rising to a small hotel. The beautiful panorama of the lake.
Standing by the landing stage are Clyde and Roberta.

9

They have just descended from the autobus.

'How pretty — how beautiful it is!' exclaims Roberta.

Eisenstein ignores the notational aspect of the scenario, and expresses the emotional quality of a scene in the free description of a writer who does not confine himself to what can be seen or heard on the screen. The result is the evocative quality of literary writing which helps the film-maker to recapture the mood of a scene when it comes to filming, and makes it good reading as literature. As notation, it is complete; it indicates not only what is to be seen and heard, but what is to be felt. Thus after Roberta's death, he describes not only Clyde's actions, but the feelings conveyed by them, indicating what is to be achieved by the actors, the director and cameraman's treatment of the location, the work of the unit as a whole :

> The sun vanishes behind the hills, behind the forest, the reflection vanishes from the lake, all becomes darker and darker.
> Through the increasing dread of the darkling forest, Clyde is making his way, his grip in his hand. He starts, alarmed by every noise, he is frightened by the cries of the night birds, he fears the moonlight penetrating between the thick branches of the trees, he fears his own shadow and the shadows of the fantastic forest.
> He desires to see the time on his watch in the moonlight, but when the lid is opened, water falls from it and he finds out that it has stopped . . .

This is carried a step further by Antonioni; in his psychological cinema, 'the whole of reality is identified with the content of consciousness, and things acquire meaning only in so far as they form part of a psychic experience' (Guido Aristarco), the meaning of things is indicated in the script, as otherwise some of the actions would not make any sense. Thus in *La notte,* in the last scene between the husband and wife:

> Lidia stops for a moment, struck once again by the

> spectacle of the cat motionlessly staring at the statue
> of a child overturned on the field. Something about
> the animal's fixedness troubles her.

The last sentence of this excerpt is a perfect illustration of
what Aristarco means. In this 'cinema of interiority', the indi-
cation of inner meaning becomes more necessary than in Eisenstein; Clyde's actions, and the emotions indicated by them are
on a single, clear, anticipatory track. If Eisenstein had made
the film it would have been remarkable not so much for the
psychological insight as for the ability to make ordinary insight spectacular and dramatic. The horse in *Strike*, the child
in *Potemkin* are symbols rather than entities in themselves;
there is no feeling expressed for the child rolling down the
steps in its perambulator, perhaps towards its death. Eisenstein shocks us by the idea rather than the fate of the individual
child; as always, he is concerned with what somebody called
'ideatic emotion', and not with Antonioni's 'content of the
consciousness' or 'interiority'. His scripts reflect this attitude
as much as Antonioni's reflect his concern for the individual. I
find the Antonioni style much nearer to literature and therefore more interesting to read. Eisenstein's style, it may be
argued, is epic but it acquires this character more in the film
than in the writing.

The pleasure of reading the film script is much greater when
it is written not only around the action, but the inner thoughts
and feelings of its characters are expressed, as in literature.
This trend has become so marked in today's cinema — even in
the work of directors as different as Satyajit Ray and Jean-Luc
Godard — that it holds out great promise for the scenario as
literature. Although Ray's style is descriptive and what one
might call linear in development, events of the mind are of
great concern to him, as in the trilogy and *Charulata* in particular. We know that Apu (*Pather Panchali*) is thinking of
his dead sister as he stands before the pond cleaning his teeth,
his fingers slowing down as the thought forms in his mind,
we know that Charu is beginning to realise the nature of her
love for her husband's brother on the swing (*Charulata*). In
writing a literary scenario — and this may not be a contradic-

tion in terms — all these unspoken thoughts may take shape. The more these unseen and unheard elements, the thoughts and feelings underlying the physical action shown, are brought out in the literary scenario, the closer it will get to the form of the novel, and become 'literature'.

But what about a scenario thus written of a film based on a novel anywhy ? Will it merely become a paraphrasing of the original novel ? I suspect not. If a close-to-novel-form scenario were to be written back from the film trilogy, a subtle transformation would take place, because it would contain something of the chemistry of the mind of the film-maker. Not only some aspects of incidents and characters, but the very composition of the elements, the molecular structure if you like, would undergo a transmutation. In the first place a film-maker is attracted to a novel because he feels an identity of thought with the writer and the content of his particular work. But given this common ground, the film-maker then proceeds to pour himself, and not the writer, into the vessel provided. Ray removes much of the dream element from Bibhuti Bhushan Bandhyopadhya's two-part novel; his Apu is a more real person than the writer's own (who turns slowly into an actual angel in *Debajan*). This happens because the creator of the films has an outlook on life, a set of mental relation-ships with the contemporary world, which are different from the writer's. Antonioni wrote the stories of all his films ex-cept one, *L'amiche;* talking about his affinities and differen-ces with Cesare Pavese, the writer, he says, 'Pavese committed suicide and I am still alive.' Pavese killed himself when he was at the height of his fame, because he felt he had come to the end of what he could accomplish. Commenting on this, Pierre Leprohn says : 'All the love Antonioni bears towards his women, all the happiness he offers them, is by contrast demanded of them by Pavese. The writer's bitterness lies in the impossibility of ever *obtaining* such happiness; for the director it seems to be the impossibility of *giving* a woman happiness.' Thus the content of a film and the novel on which it is based, although outwardly the same, become inwardly transformed.

The novel written back from the film, were such a thing to

be considered, would thus become something different from the original from which it is thrice removed. But however interesting such speculation may be, basically we are concerned here with the screenplay as literature and not the re-writing of a novel after the films based on it. The question is : can screenplays be enjoyed as literature ? I feel that it is in its distinctive form that the screenplay offers scope for a new type of literature. That form must, I think, be more than notation; it must be a completely enjoyable entity in itself, like a play read in the seclusion of the study. The problem is more difficult, in a way, in the case of those who write their own stories, as Antonioni, because the pleasure derived from it is not merely in the form; much of it must ensue from the original situations, relationship and structures brought out by the writer-half of the film-maker who creates the story. The real test lies in the case of a scenarist who adapts from a novel or a play; if he can impart to it the formal qualities, and the values of an original work in the reading itself, then the scenario can indeed become a new form of literature.

In its intimacy as well as in the sweep of the camera's observation, the inseparable audio-visual complex with its inexpressible evocation arising from a thousand details, today's art cinema in its many forms — which include such things as *cinéma vérité* — offers a challenge to literature. The films of Jean-Luc Godard, many of which are from original screenplays, present fresh problems of resolving a highly cinematic form with intricate textural qualities into a literary screenplay. Some of these problems are even more difficult than dealing with the on-the-spot newsreel-like realism of *cinéma verité;* it would be almost as difficult as describing abstract art. But the possibilities are fascinating and the challenge undeniable. Already there is a fair body of scenarios published for the reader who is familiar with film form (even if he has not seen the particular films concerned); with the growth of film appreciation, the day may not be far off when scenarios will be read as widely as plays.

1966

the documentary: art or propaganda?

Where are the blizzards? they asked Robert Flaherty, one of the creators of the documentary film, as 'The End' came to his *Moana of the South Seas* made in Samoa. Flaherty's film about the Eskimos, *Nanook of the North,* had a blizzard in it and was a best seller. They expected him to start a 'trend' with those blizzards. In the tropics, Flaherty explained, there were no blizzards. The Paramount chief remained undaunted. 'We'll send a unit down,' he said, 'and fake some.' But of course Flaherty would have none of it.

This refusal to fake is written largely across the history of the documentary's struggle for existence. The company which commissioned Flaherty to make *Nanook of the North* at first refused to accept the film : they recanted only when it became famous and brought in money. Flaherty could have then started one of those 'trends' and signed his death warrant as a maker of documentary in exchange for a highly comfortable existence. Instead, after Samoa, he went to Aran and in *Man of Aran* filmed the life of its people after living it himself for years. He captured the spirit of life of a people and the rhythm of their existence. The fight for life in the wilderness became heroic and even romantic in his vision. The art of cinema was seen at its height in the sense of intimacy, the creative editing and composition of his work.

In 1929 the greatest fighter for the documentary took the field. John Grierson made only one important film all by himself, *Drifters;* yet no one in the world has done more to raise the prestige of the documentary as an art and as a social force. *Drifters* created a sensation with its symphonic structure and its dynamic editing derived from the classic Russian school of cinema. What is more important, however, is that it initiated the entire British documentary movement and inspired such true artists as Basil Wright, Harry Watt, Cavalcanti and Paul Rotha to see life as it is and to set it forth on the screen with feeling and truth.

From the work of these men was born the one astonishing idea which has been the basis of the documentary ever since; that there can be drama without 'faking'. The documentary does not describe; it dramatizes. It does not rationalize, but creates emotions. Therefore, many like Flaherty and Ruttman and Basil Wright argued that the documentary was an art. The materialists of the world argued that, for the same reason, the documentary was an instrument of persuasion, a part of the election campaign, the grow-more-food campaign, the drink-more-tea campaign and many other campaigns. So the question was asked, as it still is : Is the documentary art or propaganda?

But the subject of cinema — feature or documentary — is life, and the reality of life can be expressed in many ways. In their extreme forms, feature and documentary can become pure fiction or strict record. But in practice it is difficult for them to be either. Writing on the excellent Crown Unit documentary, *Coastal Command,* C. A. Lejeune says:

> In common with other documentary producers, however, Crown has one characteristic that chills me. There is detachment in much of its work, an almost scandalized mistrust of showmanship, an effort, it would seem to avoid, not only melodramatics, but any form of human appeal or persuasion. It would be unacceptable, I feel, to speak too warmly of a Crown Unit film. Crown does not want our affection. It only wants our respect.
>
> The unemotional approach would doubtless be excused on the grounds that the official recorder is presenting history, not drama. It is this fallacy, into which so many eminent historians have fallen, that has helped to make the past in the main such a dead letter. All

records, even photographic records, are a matter of selection and viewpoint and into every record of fact there must enter at some time the creative impulse of the interpreter. The best and liveliest historians are those who can convey the feeling of a scene to later generations. For emotion, whether of fear or excitement, elation or impatience, or even a nervous and fretful triviality, is as much a part of any historical event as the deeds done or the people involved in them. Without some hint of this intangible quality, some ghost of a message from one human heart to another, no record, however factual, can be either truthful or complete.

('The Documentalists Dilemma' in *Chestnuts in Her Lap*, Phoenix, U.S.A.: 1947, pp. 83-84.)

In support of Lejeune's plea one might relate a scene from the Czech documentary *Life from out of the Ruins*. The workers lay rails over a broken bridge which they have just reconstructed with great difficulty and stand back and wait as the first train rumbles up the rebuilt bridge. Music is high while the workers are at their work, but as the train approaches the bridge all sound is suddenly cut off; the sounds of the wheels on the rails, of water below the bridge, of the voice of the men are gone; in the tense silence the commentator whispers the question which is in every heart : 'Will it hold ?' Then there is silence again broken only by the intermittent hiss of the engine as it steams up, which seems to echo the whisper. As the engine reaches the other bank, all the sounds come back, the tension relaxes and the music sweeps the emotions forward to a powerful climax. The artistic use of sound creates here a tense suspense which belongs more to the feature film than to the documentary.

The utilitarian aspect of the documentary has gained considerable ground in recent years. Governments and commercial organizations tend more and more to make it the slave of their immediate needs. To many, the original (but not etymological) meaning of the word 'documentary' has become indistinguishable from the newsreel film, the educational film, the scientific film and the publicity film. Any film made from natural material is dubbed 'documentary'. Feature-producers speak of 'documentary shots' if they happen to include the scene of a cotton mill shot from real life mainly because of the high costs of faking it.

A film is not documentary according to the label under which it is shipped, but according to its style and emphasis, according to the spirit of realism which informs it. Thus even a feature film can have a documentary outlook on life, as recent Italian films like Rossellini's *Paisa,* De Sica's *Shoeshine* and *Bicycle Thieves* are reported to have. The art of the documentary lies in a power to create emotions and patterns from actual life, thus interpreting it in a creative manner. It it, therefore, in some ways, a more difficult art than the feature film. Its much discussed 'creative treatment of actuality' lies in the style rather than in the story. It cannot arrange the material of life to create artistic designs and movements but must discover them in life as it is. Its freedom is strictly limited; there are no artistic distortions, no departure from fact to deepen feeling. The interest it must create to hold its audience has to be based on art alone.

Occasionally a romantic documentary of the Flaherty-type might charm an audience with its unfamiliar world; but the effect, even in Flaherty, is not derived from the emotional potentialities of the story, and in some of the most exciting films of ordinary life, much less so. Indeed it might be said that the height of documentary art is seen only where it creates emotion out of — perhaps seemingly — abstract patterns, out of rhythm and movement, almost independently of the subject. The best documentary must be pure cinema, which is a sort of visual music. Like music, it must be movement in time, with each image like a note in music, related to other notes, inevitably. There are scenes in the British colour documentary *Steel* (Ronald Riley; photographed by Jack Cardiff) which fill us with a sense of awe, created purely by visual means by treating the subject in terms of colour and mass, line and movement. Red-hot lengths of steel leap forward like tongues of fire across machinery looming in the dark; through a giant gate shaped like a five-pointed star the red mass rolls down; streaks of red dance about in the darkness, weaving arabesques of beauty.

In *Night Mail* (Harry Watt and Basil Wright) the rails become shining blades of steel, ever broadening out, turning, joining, issuing out of one another in a zigzag pattern of speeding out lines; the train tears through the darkness of the night, shattering the silence with its overwhelming uproar. The creative use of image, sound and movement makes the postal train a living dramatic character. Its workers with their profiles still in the darkness in contrast to the orgy of movement, become living human beings, and their common labour assumes heroic proportions.

In their proselytizing zeal the rulers of the destiny of documentary — for documentaries must be subsidized — are apt to forget that the documentary owes its persuasive power to its effectiveness as art. They harness the documentary to their campaigns and leave the art to take care of itself. Thus, too often, the documentary becomes a mere propaganda vehicle for the political, social or educational views of those who pull its financial strings.

The strength and weakness of the documentary as an art lies in its purposive nature. Another complicating factor is that it does not pay its way but must be subsidized by government or other organizations. Both these reasons combine to burden the documentary with more messages than it can bear. The utilitarian attitude to documentary is most marked in India where the art of film generally is undeveloped. The feature has been left to its own low horseplay; the documentary is being taken up as the battle-axe of social reform. Visual education has become almost a magic phrase. There is a great legend about its achievements in the West and great things are expected from it here. It is almost as if there will be a regeneration in the country if only some documentary films, of any standard, are shown every week in every village.

It is important to remember here that the documentary depends for its educative power on its dramatic effectiveness, that is, on its effectiveness as art. Perhaps it is better not to show any documentary to our people than to show bad ones.

The present cry for visual education might die out if bad specimens prevent the documentary from proving its worth. It is not enough to produce good photography, music and editing, all of which the present output of the Films Division provides; what we need is a better and more creative attitude to the documentary. What the Films Division and other able documentary units in India (like the DUI in Bombay) lack is inspiration and also artistic integrity. While the camera eye is growing more and more perfect, the mind behind the camera is dull and, at its best, merely competent.

This lack of inspiration is due largely to what I have described above as the utilitarian outlook. The documentary is profoundly social in its implications; yet there is a need to free it from the burdens of journalistic immediateness of purpose in order to allow it to be an art. The function of the documentary, as Grierson said, is 'to wake the heart and the will', not the sinews. Once the heart is awakened the sinews must follow in the end. There is a natural honesty in the documentary outlook, and it is enough if people understand the problems and are not spoonfed with solutions advocated by the party in power.

It is also important to remember that although the documentary is most often made in order to persuade, it can never hope to influence the lives of people to the extent of the feature film which has entertainment as its ostensible aim. The importance of cinema as a social force in our age is due almost entirely to the spell which the illusory world of the feature film exercises over its vast audience. Research has shown that the influence of the entertainment film enters deep into the social and moral life of our day and moulds our habits and manners and ways of thought in a far more serious fashion than we are prepared to believe. For the feature film sets forth that image of essential reality which lies under appearances; through illusion it creates a dream correlative of reality in which the conflicts and emotional problems of real life are resolved and harmonized. When the mind returns to actuality after this excitation of deeper self-consciousness, it retains an amount of the equilibrium it acquires from the resolution of conflict in the dream world. The Greeks understood this principle of catharsis and practised it in their drama in good, bad and indifferent ways, and the film, a young art, is no exception.

There may be, and indeed is, much that is evil in the influence of the feature film today due to the commercial nature of film production. For all we know, a generation grown on Bombay-made films may be unable one day to make love to its girls without a tree to hang from and a memory for song hits. But the fact remains that all over the world millions of people see feature films every day and derive something from them which they do not derive from anything else. The feature film, the most universal art of today, performs a psychological service for the masses from which the other arts retired long ago. This service is seen at its highest form in a film like Chaplin's *Gold Rush* (1924) with its many levels of appeal, one leading to the other at its lowest, in the cheap Hollywood 'leg-show' musical. The documentary increases the fund of knowledge creatively, without turning the mind into a mere godown of information; but it cannot portray the human 'soul'. For that fantasy and illusion are absolutely essential. Thus the influence of the fictional film is in general much deeper than that of the documentary. This is largely true even in India where the level of feature film-making is one of the very worst in the world.

It should thus appear that our leaders should adopt a policy in favour of putting more sense and human feeling into the Indian feature film and allow the documentary to lead a less missionary existence. What I am driving at is a more balanced development of feature and documentary, resulting in the development of the cinema as an art and as a social force. The documentary is also an art and the feature has also tremendous social force; so it will not do to ignore one and press on with the other on the score of the educational value of the documentary.

But the development of the documentary, which the government has already taken in hand, is further needed for its chastening effect which will clear the air of the musty staleness, the theatrical cobwebs and the sentimental heaviness of the Indian feature film. To bring health and freshness to it, one must take the camera out to the streets and slums and villages of India and take stock of real life in the proper documentary manner. This will mean the growth of only the very realistic feature film for a time, but that will have to be tolerated for the sake of the general good. The late renaissance in British films was largely due to the British tradition in documentary emotionalized by the tensions of the war. The character of the prewar British feature film was so similar in many ways to that of our present feature output that a similar effect of the documentary on feature films in India is not beyond the range of possibilities.

The first requisite of such an effect, as of all other effects of the documentary, will have to be the birth of a truly creative outlook on the documentary. There is too much sameness in our work, too little energy and inspiration. Indeed it is almost impossible to distinguish between the work of various units without the help of the credit titles. Most of the work is modelled on Western documentary types, and little attempt is made to find a style suitable for India. Competence is poor consolation in a country so vast and colourful as ours and so full of peoples and traditions. In our tribal areas and ancient ruins, in the spectacular festivals and the ordinary life of our people there are many *Nanooks* and *Moanas* waiting to be revealed — to ourselves and to the world.

1949

films remembered

It is astonishing to think of the number of films one sees in the course of a few years. For many people it is usual to see one every week, which makes it, say, fifty every year. In twenty years this adds up to about one thousand feature films, and probably five thousand shorts.

How many does one remember out of this vast number of films ? It is a disturbing thought that one remembers so few. Disturbing because one of the tests of the worth of film, as of any experience, is whether it is remembered. It is not enough, of course, to recall a title or the name of a star. What one should remember is, surely, the experience. For most people, I suppose, this takes the form of certain vivid images which stand out in the memory and which in their turn evoke the emotions and feelings they had once aroused.

For those who take a lively interest in the cinema, the classics are easy enough to remember. They are talked about and written about so much that I would rather leave out the *Gold Rushes* and *Potemkins.* They are like the classics of literature. You might study them for the examinations or read them for delight, but forget them you cannot. When you are associated with the work of film societies, you see them over and over again. I have seen *Potemkin* perhaps fifteen times, but thanks again to the Calcutta Film Society, I have seen many other good, if not classic, films outside the commercial cinema. Adding to these the much larger number seen in the commercial cinema, reminiscing becomes as difficult as it is delightful.

In the early days of the Calcutta Film Society was screened

Jagirdar's *Ramshastri,* which is one of the best historical films I have seen. It had a period feeling, exciting but natural action, and a sobriety of sentiment which distinguished it from the rest of Indian cinema of that period. I shall not forget the tense face and the flaring nostrils of Lalita Pawar in the close-ups. The film was directed with a quiet sureness of touch without any self-conscious artiness, and although its technique had nothing strikingly novel about it, it avoided the common pitfalls of exaggeration and was singularly apt. I found it better than Sohrab Modi's *Sikander,* which I saw soon after but which was devoid of any true content behind its pompous exterior.

Talking about Hollywood historicals, however, an untypical one I remember is Wilhelm Dieterle's *Juarez* with Paul Muni, which made a strong impression on me at the time. Paul Muni's characterization of Juarez's iron-clad personality contrasted powerfully with the charm of Maximilian and somehow underlined the inevitability of historical events, although the film seemed to have no political attitudes. Most memorable of all, however, are Eisenstein's *Ivan the Terrible* and *Alexander Nevsky,* both acted by the great Nikolai Cherkassov.

Eisenstein is the only film director who found a true excitement in the sheer scale and magnificence of the historical film, and had the largeness of imagination, the power of technique and the sense of history to express it fully. In Cherkassov he had the dream actor of god-like appearance and sonorous voice whose range of acting ability becomes clear in the contrast between Nevsky and Ivan on the one hand and Don Quixote on the other. The enormity of the canvas, the sense of design, the larger-than-life quality of Alexander Nevsky must remain a memorable achievement in an otherwise straightforward film. *Ivan the Terrible* in two parts is a far more complicated work, which in exploring history also explores the mind of an individual to an extent and on a scale never before attempted, and never since. But then I am again taking the short-cut of the 'classics'...

If the choice lay between a bad social film and a bad Western, which one would you see? I would see the Western any day. This may be regarded as snobbish, but then the worst Western has some interesting landscape, splendid horses and plenty of action. The men are sometimes no better than the horses, but they are fast with their guns, and when a Western is good it is delightful. Take Fred Zinnemann's *High Noon* for instance. For unity of time, place and action, atmosphere, tension and poetry, few films equal it. Remember the song 'Do not forsake me, oh my darling'? Between the vocal and instrumental variations the song provides the complete musical score of the film, again helping its unity. The photography, too, with its sharp contrast of light and shadow, perfectly depicts the atmosphere of high noon. You always know, more or less, what is going to happen in a Western. You knew, for instance, that in the end Gary Cooper was going to kill all the bandits and get back his girl. Yet you were interested to the end not to see what happened, but how it happened, and whenever the accent in a film is on how it happens rather than on what, the chances are that it should be good.

As Jean Renoir once said, if you asked everyone to make films on the same subject, you would quickly find out who was an artist and who was not. The search for novel stories is, thus, more often than not, an attempt to hide the emptiness of the direction behind the glamour of the subject. Take John Ford's Westerns for sheer contrast. The stories have the classic simplicity of the true Western, yet most of the films from *Stagecoach* to *Wagonmaster* have a poetry that delights the eye and the ear and they communicate something of the courage with which the early immigrants built up the 'new country'. Clashes were unavoidable in the conglomeration of races and communities out of which the United States of America emerged. *Stagecoach* set a pattern which in all these years has hardly changed. It has perennial appeal. To me, one of the finest of Ford's Westerns was *Fort Apache* in which he turns the clatter of horses' hoofs into music and the foul language of Henry Fonda, as the choleric army officer, into poetry. Ford's handling of virile action is as exciting as his observation of character and landscape is poetic. Besides, in a film like *The Searchers*, he has a deep awareness of what the white man was doing to the Indian. It takes a director of great ability to achieve this combination.

Every good Hollywood director turns to the Western from time to time as a sure-fire box-office subject from which the artist is free to extract all visual and aural delight that he is capable of. I have already mentioned Zinnemann, who is so well known for his creation of other types of film such as *The Search*. William Wellman made a memorable Western in *Yellow Sky* with Gregory Peck. The picture of the four horsemen appearing on the horizon of hard, glittering desert country, of the tension as the girl appears among the men while they drink water at a tank alongside their horses, is unforgettable. Again the poetry is built on landscape, the handsome gracefulness of the horses, the tension of isolation from society, the simple courage and, what is more, the bold sketches of character.

William Wyler, who made a fine film out of Henry James's preciously perfect story in *The Heiress* and charmed everyone with *Friendly Persuasion,* made *The Big Country,* a strangely moving Western not of war but of peace. Can anyone forget the scene of Gregory Peck being beaten in the wilderness or the fight in the twilight between him and Heston, filmed constantly in comical long-shot ? George Stevens made *Shane* — another memorable Western — not long before *Giant* which is so different in its story. Director after director returns to the simplicity of the Western probably to renew his touch with the earthiness and vigour of the Western, which lends fresh strength to his style and a boldness to his concepts.

When Uday Shankar's *Kalpana* was released in Calcutta, the film society mailed tickets for the first show to all members, and soon after the show we had a very pompous discussion. We agreed that although the dancing and the music were very good, and presented in cinematic style, the film as a whole was poor. I was one of those who vociferously proclaimed this opinion, yet I saw *Kalpana* at least eight times in a row and know of others, notably Satyajit Ray, who saw it probably a dozen times. *Kalpana* ran for twenty-six weeks in one cinema in Calcutta. It is a testimony to the appeal of

10

the musical film when it has real music in it. Despite the banal story, the lapses in taste, the mawkish sentimentality and the cliché-ridden 'philosophy', *Kalpana* had a musical grandeur.

Uday Shankar understood the medium of the cinema to the extent of sacrificing the continuity and movement of his dance to the continuity and movement of his film. This is what gave *Kalpana* its basic appeal which would probably have vanished if he had filmed each dance number straight from start to finish. Many musicals have since been made but none has achieved the status of *Kalpana*.

Baiju Bawra had its moments, but its story was still worse, and its compromise in music too vulgar to have any sustained appeal at all. Satyajit Ray's *Jalsaghar* has some magnificent musical passages, well related to the action and the mode of the story, but it can hardly be called a musical film. In fact, the only trouble about this otherwise haunting film is that it cannot make up its mind on what it wants to be. It tries to be a pure poem of mood and nostalgia, a musical and an essay on the decay of feudalism, all at the same time.

The delightful musicals all seem to come from the West. From *Top Hat* (1935) to *Daddy Long Legs* (1955) Fred Astaire danced away with complete abandon on the tight rope between the classical and the cabaret, always infectiously gay, yet always in good taste. Meanwhile, Astaire's wit, charm and sophistication, his lively numbers and his expert choreography put America at the top for musicals. This was kept up and bettered by Gene Kelly's still more free, intelligent and masculine personality and his irresistible sense of rhythm. It was exciting to see *On the Town, Singing in the Rain, An American in Paris*. A youthful, healthy charm and gaiety makes it impossible to outgrow these films. An enchanting musical was Stanley Donen's *The Pajama Game*. Its title number has certainly the most beautifully photographed musical sequence ever seen. Shot outdoors, this picnic sequence with the trees, the water and the costumes almost fluorescent, made one colour-drunk, as it were. Another outstanding memory is of the Russian *Romeo and Juliet* with Ulanova. Despite Ulanova's age, so obvious in the close-ups, the film weaves a web of enchantment in colour, period, costume, exciting choreography and music. It turns pure ballet into cinema without making very much fuss about the transformation.

The musical leads me inevitably to the subject of comedy. What is the timing of Chaplin except a form of dance? His genius for hitting the wrong thing at the wrong moment has a perfect rhythm. For once, two or more wrongs make a right. His very gait is musical, so are his moods of friskiness and sulking, punctuated by outburst of merriment, accompanied by the swinging stick and the wobbing hat, like the allegros and scherzos of a soloist. The ever-turning door from which he cannot escape, the streamers that he eats with his spaghetti, are all ruled by a rhythm of his own world.

To me even words sound like music when in *Monsieur Verdoux* he hides under the table from the policeman who bends down and asks : 'What are you looking for ?'

Chaplin: 'A sandwich.'

Policeman: 'What kind of sandwich?'

Chaplin: 'An ordinary sandwich — a piece of bread between two slices of meat.'

In this situation on the eve of his capture, Chaplin's most ordinary words become so expressive that they attain the status of music, suggesting the inexpressible with their very ordinariness.

But even before he deigned to speak, even before his character had finally become the symbol of the have-not, his comedy had great power — the power to make you laugh. Only a few years ago I saw *The Champion* (1915) and realised anew Chaplin's sheer genius as a clown, tragic or otherwise. As he fought his unequal fights with boxers of every description, the laughter rose in spirals within you, widening out until it spilt your sides and you nearly choked on it. He is cunning enough to know just when you can laugh no more, when your senses become too numb to react. It is then that he gives you your much-needed pause, perhaps a thoroughly sentimental one. Then it starts again. There is more laughter in those two reels of primitive film-making than in the entire history of the film comedy outside Chaplin. Compared to him, the Marx Brothers' pranks seem terribly adult, in spite of all one hears about their innocence.

But then every great comedian beckons you into his own private world, and once you enter it, he absorbs you slowly but surely until you do just as he tells you. He may not be as great as the other one, but while you are with him, you are under his spell. The Marx Brothers' world is a strange place where anything can happen. The three are actually one, with three faces. The silent Harpo is at the root of the mischief, supplying all the motive power of destruction with his complete unawarness of the adult world. Groucho puts it into words and makes it absurd by looking as grown-up as anyone possibly could. Chicko provides the link between the frothy surface and the speechless world below, where only music makes any sense. For me, the best of the Marxes was in *Go West, The Big Store, A Night at the Opera,* in each of which their sublime innocence wreaks such complete havoc on the world of logic.

A step nearer to that world, but still reasonably far from it in *The Secret Life of Walter Mitty,* was Danny Kaye. Danny Kaye later turned rather insipid, but in *Walter Mitty,* there was never a dull moment. Like all good caricatures it made us laugh because it exaggerated only the truth. Perhaps no man is a hero to himself. Walter Mitty is an absurd amalgam of all the things one would like to do to people to whom one must submit. The film brought out something we all had bottled up inside us without being aware of it. I think in that one film Danny Kaye expressed himself completely, so completely that his later ones have not much to express.

Clifton Webb, a much commoner soul, struck a true note for once in *Sitting Pretty,* where the pompousness of the intellectual is so funny to inhabitants of the day-to-day world that they let him get away with it. But the audience let him get away with it only once, for such comedians depend solely on new gags, and every new gag becomes old, it becomes particularly difficult when there is only one gag. *Sitting Pretty* expressed something; its sequels merely copied its one gag with a killing boredom. But the audience is never killed, it simply moves on; it is the gag that dies.

The theatrical comedy, the comedy of manners, has succeeded on the screen now and then but never left any indelible stamp. Whether it is *Pygmalion* or *The Reluctant Debutante*, it may make us laugh, but it leaves us no poorer without it. It is the immortal comedian who expresses something deeper than words, whether an anguish or a complete innocence, or a revolt that lives in our memory. To me it is the comedian and not the situation that makes the comedy. How sadly lacking we have been in true comedy in India!

The unspeakable grotesquerie that passes in the name of comedy in India is something that should be banned by the S.P.C.A. The only Indian comedy I have seen, if you can call it one, is Satyajit Ray's *Parash Pather*. Tulsi Chakravorty has an undoubted comic gift, but characterstically enough Satyajit turns his performance into a tragic-comic expression, in which there is more of the tragic than the comic. It moved one and made one laugh, sometimes it did both at the same time, as in the scene where Tulsi Chakravorty realises that he has the touchstone, starts to laugh, and then his laughter turns into tears. Alas, such moments were few; most of the time laughter and tears both remained effective but separate. Nevertheless it was amazing to find that the director of *Pather Panchali* was capable of such humour.

Although by no means a comedy, Ritwik Ghatak's *Ajantrik* contains a sequence of macabre humour in the opening, where an imbecile bridegroom accompanied by an obese uncle travels through a beautiful countryside in a ramshackle car driven by a near lunatic. The near lunatic later turns out to be a very human character, drawn with a deep sense of humanity. But that is another story.

Or is it? For *Ajantrik* is one of the many films which refuse to take a label and yet leaves a mark on the memory. Anything that does not fit into a category we in India lump together as 'social' films. The label is correct only in so far as such films deal with society, as all films do, except those about talking mules and the like. In style and in content, *Ajantrik* is remarkable, and different. An uneven, eccentric work, its images are memorable, its treatment fully cinematic. Ritwik Ghatak has a definite feeling for people and places, and a great eye for the camera. *Ajantrik* is a somewhat avant-garde film about man's emotional relationship to machines in a primitive economy which is coming into contact with large-scale industry for the first time.

The basic motivation behind Satyajit Ray's films is not very different, though I see in them a nostalgia for one's country, an urge to rediscover it, to identify oneself with it and feel that one belongs to it. Such a nostalgia is created by the wide gulf that divides the English-educated upper middle class from the vast masses of the people within the same country. Yet Ray's approach to art is deeply Indian: it is melodic rather than dramatic, concerned with eternal human values rather than immediate phenomena, inclined towards the continuum of life rather than the conflict of life and death. That is why there is a sense of resignation and a fatalism in his treatment of death, as if it were a part of the process of life. The only film which I find jarring in parts in this context is *Jalsaghar*. In the scene of the boy's death, or even the zamindar's own (to a lesser extent), the manner of realisation does not seem to bear out Ray's intent.

There are some films which one remembers independently of one's judgement. Such a one is Marcel Carné's *Les Enfants du paradis*. I saw it three times during the International Film Festival in 1952, which took some doing. It was perhaps decadent, certainly sentimental, and hopelessly romantic, but it was pure enchantment, such as only a dream can offer. Jean-Louis Barrault's clown, white-faced as if with an icy mask of death from which the eyes look on steadily, craving life and love; Arletty's stillness, broken only by a slight movement of the head or the hand or the eyes; the world apparently bustling with life, but inwardly feeling lost, a world in which even Arletty's fickle love somehow seems so valuable, so reminiscent of life. An inexpressible sadness lies beneath the surface gaiety, much as in the life of occupied France where the film was made.

Almost all films treat the subject of love in some form or another, but some do so more than others, particularly when you consider sexual love. One hears and sees and reads of nothing but 'love' on records, on the air, in the cinema and the

restaurant, in books and plays. 'Love' assails you from all
directions all the time; the world, it would seem, is full of
'love'. Perhaps it is because the world is so full of hatred,
ruthless selfishness and violence, that protestations of love
fill the air. It is only painters who seem so refreshingly free
of it, content to paint a piece of orange or a tree, or a man
with a hat in his hand; even when they paint a nude they
are busy in distorting the body so that sexual love is the last
thing it makes you think of. Films are at the other end of
the pole; they live on 'love'. The falseness and banality of
90 per cent of the cinema's output of 'love' is simply shattering. Love is the cinema's most easily manufactured, most
saleable commodity.

That is why when, once in a while, it rings true, as in the
clown's love for the leading lady (a very familiar subject) in
Les Enfants du paradis, one experiences the relief of coming
across the real thing in a mass of perfectly manufactured paper
flowers, complete with the right perfume. Many good films
have been made on themes of war, the Wild West, laughter,
music, goldhunt, childhood, adventure, and so on; very few
on the specific theme of sexual love. Few good directors
dare attempt it; they prefer to use suggestions of it in films
mainly occupied with other themes. Carol Reed's *The Third
Man,* for instance, or *Odd Man Out,* were both hauntingly
beautiful films in which love is in the background as a real,
powerful force most of the time, and is brought to the fore
only at the very end.

Rarely has anyone attempted such a straightforward film on
the subject of love as David Lean in *Brief Encounter.* Consider
the difficulties the film sets itself; it takes a contented, middle-
aged, unimpressive looking man and a contended, middle-
aged, unimpressive looking woman, and makes them fall in
love. Nothing really 'happens' between them, for before it
does they go back to their own marriages in the interest of all
concerned. The director denies himself all the easy ways
out. It has no surging passions to the accompaniment of
screaming violins, no triangles, no duels, no verbal gymnastics.
It is moving because it is real. The film has a perfect form,
with a unity of time, place and action. The unspoken thoughts

of the woman used as commentary are one of the most
effective devices. Yet it is used with such delicacy and blends
so well with the rest of the technique that one is never aware
of it as device. *Brief Encounter* is the best 'love film' I have
seen to date.

What is the opposite of love — crime or war ? In a sense
both may be the same, but let us deal with crime first. Here
is another popular subject of the cinema, but one in which
success has come oftener than in the case of love. The reason
is that crime films are more concerned with outward events
and do not face the difficult problem of making human relationships seem true. Take Hitchcock's films — brilliantly
contrived, masterly in technique, but the characters are like
cut-outs; they merely fulfil a function. It is not a drama of
people, but of situations. Only rarely do the characters emerge
as real human beings as, to some extent, in his *Strangers on
a Train.*

I have not seen the German or early Hollywood work of
Fritz Lang, another master of suspense, but his later work certainly seems no more interested in human beings than Hitchcock's. All I remember are my reactions to *Ministry of Fear,*
more icy in its suggestions of unknown danger than any other
film I have seen. It is in Robert Siodmak's *Cry of the City* that
there was genuine feeling for the criminal (Richard Conte),
even on the part of the policeman (Victor Mature) who tracks
him down. It was, at the same time, a fine piece of suspense
drama, realistic in photography and in the staging of action.
It was crime drama which not only kept you on the edge of
your seat but touched a deeper chord within you. I much pre-
ferred it to that overrated herald of realism — *Naked City.*

It is not surprising that all the good crime films one can
remember are Hollywood's. Crime is Hollywood's forte;
others who have copied Hollywood have only shown their in-
eptitude, our own *C.I.D*'s being the most banal imitations.

War is probably the true opposite of love, for most of the
good films on it have been made to disapprove of it. But
whether they speak in sorrow or in anger, war films provide
an opportunity for first-rate movie-making, sensational in pictures and sounds. Even Milestone's *All Quiet on the Western*

Front, that classic indictment of war, is a delight to the eye and the ear in its brilliant fighting sequences. It realises the sensations of war better than many later war films, while at the same time it is more serious in intent.

A Czech film I remember vividly was Otakar Vavra's *Silent Barricade,* which was properly patriotic, but produced the visual and aural sensations in a very inventive and original manner. A man walks along a deserted street with a load on his back. Suddenly the silence is broken by a volley of shots fired from off screen and holes appear on his load like a battery of lights switched on one by one, in quick succession.

An otherwise unimpressive Soviet war film — *Rainbow* — was made remarkable only by a sound, the sound of a friendly aeroplane. Its drone approaches from the distance and gradually fills the ear, bringing a message of hope across the blue sky of terrors and making a turning point in the film with its melody. It is one of the most perfect, most musical uses of a sound effect that I can remember.

By comparison the inventions of David Lean's *Bridge on the River Kwai* seem so brittle in their cleverness. With all its highly intriguing plot, its deft direction, exotic setting and expert acting, the *Bridge*'s condemnation of war seems only a pose, an exit line on the 'madness' of war necessary to round off the film. Yet David Lean's film cannot be dismissed lightly, it is too clever, too expertly planned and executed not to leave a distinct mark on the memory.

Somehow, war and aeroplanes bring to mind another film of David Lean's — *The Sound Barrier.* The ground sequences are adequately pedestrian — I do not know what he sees in Ann Todd — but the action in the air is superbly captured. It is thrilling: it is a feast for the senses. The sounds have a rare tension and power and the pictures a true suggestion of the infinite that beckons to man. For the sheer delights of war (on celluloid!) the action sequences of *The Bridges of Toko-Ri* also ring in the ears.

From war to costume drama and swashbuckling adventure, rich in visual beauty, is not as far a cry as it may seem. There is the same incisiveness of pace and vividness of image in Akira Kurosawa's *Rashomon* as Toshiro Mifune prowls through the forest, the blade of his axe burning in the strong sunlight filtering through the leaves. But there is more in *Rashomon* than just pace and vividness. Its enigmatic story, its images of haunting loveliness and bizarre, supernatural fantasy, its counterpoint of heroism and cowardice, delicacy and barbaric force, weave a rich texture of thoughts, feelings and sensations.

Do you remember the scene in which the medium sits in the middle of the courtyard, bathed in sunlight, dressed in white flowing robes, backed by a long, straight line of black shadow? There is a plant in front of the ghostly figure in white, and as the woman speaks out with the voice of the dead man, there is a gust of wind, and the plant sways in one direction, the woman's flowing robe in another, producing an eerie feeling of the supernatural.

Rashomon is a Shakespearean work on the flickleness of woman and the dilemma of a man in which the only character which shines in a clear light free from equivocation, fearless as a tiger, is the bandit. The role is inconceivable without the magnificent Toshiro Mifune, who must be one of the greatest actors in present-day cinema.

We are getting close to the subject of fantasy, and I cannot but mention one of my favourite films full of a rare delicacy — Jean Cocteau's *La Belle et la bete.* If *Rashomon* blends the real and the unreal, so does *La Belle et la bete,* although in a completely different way and for a different purpose. It is the measure of his genius that Cocteau, whom Renoir described to us as 'a strange man, even in France', brings off such a fine achievement in the cinema as an interlude in his complex preoccupations with painting, plays and poetry. The hens cackle and the sisters fight; a girl looks into the mirror and sees a monkey instead of herself. In the midst of the simple, everyday life, a secret door opens into a fantastic world of dark places, disembodied hands holding lighted candles, and strange beasts, eerie silences. I do not care so much for the moral ending towards which Cocteau strives, as for the path along which he approaches it. Was he suggesting that the fascist beast had a heart inside, which could be won with love? Or, that all obstacles can be overcome if we have purity of the soul? I do not know, and do not care.

But one must call a halt to this long, rambling and hopelessly incomplete reminiscence. If anything has emerged from
it, it is that in a good film the subject matters least; what matters is the intensity of feeling for life and truth of expression
that one achieves. Whether it is a film of war or of peace,
of love or of crime, whether it is comic or tragic, realistic or
fantastic, the only thing of value is the experience of life that
a film, like any other art, brings to us. Unfortunately in the
present state of film appreciation in India, it is still necessary
to spell this out in so many words. If subject matter was not
the main determinant for those who sit in judgement on the
cinema, how does one account for the President's Gold Medal
for *Shyamchi Aie* or *Kabuliwala* ?

1960

cinema in the sixties: some trends

Film festivals, art theatres, and film societies all over the world have grown today to an extent which brings together the minority audience of all countries in a new bond of internationality despite the barrier of language. The hiatus between the 'art film' and the commercial cinema has widened; there is much less in common between *Hiroshima mon amour* and *Hercules* than there was between *Birth of a Nation* and *Quo Vadis.* The artistic film has lost the big audiences of Chaplin and Ford, but what it has lost at home it has gained abroad. Had it not been for this new international audience, films like Antonioni's *La notte* or Bunuel's *Viridiana* could hardly have been made, and the sound film would have been totally condemned to commercialism. The eggheads of the cinema have clubbed together to provide an international audience even to the most esoteric national product. Kurosawa's *Rashomon* did not win much kudos in Japan, but the Grand Prix at Venice brought it to light before the minority audiences of the world, and not only made it their firm favourite but created a new international interest in the Japanese cinema as a whole.

Yet this new internationality in cinema in the sound period has not made serious films less national in character but more so than ever. It has become a trite saying that the more national the cinema becomes, the more international is its acceptance; to the extent that Japanese or Indian films that show the Westernised middle class are generally less favoured in Europe than what expresses the traditional. The cinema has become, more than ever before, a major means for one country to get to know the mind of another. The world of the cinema has become a closer, smaller world.

The film director as an artist today enjoys far greater freedom than did his predecessors. Griffith and Chaplin had a Shakespearean genius for making a virtue of a necessity, of making their peace with a massive audience; nevertheless Chaplin failed with *Woman of Paris* and never again strayed from the straight and the narrow. Today a film like *Paris nous appartient* is patiently borne by festival gatherings and gets booked in the art theatre circuit, for the audience is prepared to see it merely to keep itself informed even without enjoying it. It is the audience which, in this circuit, has a duty to the film director. As an art it has been the answer of the cinema to the challenge of television, while as commerce it has given itself up to spectacle. Jean Renoir used to predict that eventually television would take out all the rubbish from the cinema and leave it a purer art. As far as the big screen which became the commercial cinema's answer to television is concerned, Jean Cocteau's comment sums up the reaction of the artist succinctly: 'Next time I write a poem,' he said, 'it will be on a big sheet of paper.'

With this new-found freedom, the cinema in the West (where the minority audience is most developed) has become more and more personal in its expression. Eisenstein had been free enough to make far-reaching experiments with form; but when he tried to express himself in content as in *Ivan the Terrible*, he got into serious trouble. Russia banned *Bezhin Meadow*, American would not let him complete *Que Viva Mexico*. Neither country was in doubt about his artistic ability; yet one restrained his content for political, and the other for commercial, reasons. Today the recognition of the film director's right to express himself is so great that Sjoman's *491* is allowed to ride roughshod over the protest of the majority of the Swedish public. It is a film about juvenile delinquents in which the inmates of a modern reformatory school, enraged by their loss of faith in the only teacher who truly cared for them, take out their frustration on the nearest available woman by making her copulate with a dog. It is a highly moral and deeply human film, but its manner of confronting the audience with reality is so brutal that it raised howls of protest which the Swedish government chose to ignore.

Humanism has been an essential part of serious cinema as much as of serious literature. Social protest has been its major theme. But the humanism of Renoir or Mizoguchi, Pudovkin or even De Sica was what might be called 'objective humanism'. It followed the broad, accepted, socially hallowed lines of humanism firmly laid down in advance by literature. Compared to it, the concern for the human being felt by Bergman or Fellini, Antonioni or Resnais and Truffaut originates far more from within the artist himself. *Hiroshima mon amour* is as concerned with humanity as *La Grande Illusion;* but Resnais' film is not grand passion over a great cause — it has a deeply personal intensity which reaches inward rather than out towards the world. In the *Childhood of Ivan* Tarkovsky shows us the life of a child during the war, a little spy wading through moors in the moonlight, under the shadow of tall trees, a child who never knew childhood. What a far cry it is from, say, Pudovkin's *Mother!* Chukhrai's young soldier in *Ballad of a Soldier* is a similar portrait of innocence caught in meshes of war — an attitude so different from Dovzhenko's *Shore* or *Arsenal.* Even in Russia, they have tired of striking patriotic attitudes, of the national hero covering himself with glory in the service of socialism and motherland. Poland reassessed its heroes brutally in *Kanal* and *Ashes and Diamonds,* exposing the tired individuals behind the heroic mask, trying to find a purpose behind their deeds. Antonioni's *La notte* again seeks meaning in the life of the individual, his loneliness, his endless effort to find a worthwhile relationship with his surroundings, and some value in himself. From *Seventh Seal* to *Silence,* Bergman despairs of mankind in a godless world empty of all faith. In the mid-sixties, it looks as though the day of the social cause is definitely over in the cinema.

There are so few social causes left in the Europe of today. In the hundred years since Marx, the material uplift of the masses was the motivating force behind a lot of art, endowing it with a heroic purpose. In capitalism and communism alike that purpose has been largely achieved. Life in most countries is insured from birth to death. A Buddha let loose in

Copenhagen could not moan over the *material* woes of man. A Dickens could hardly find the poorhouses to describe, even if he took a plane to Crete. On the other hand there are clashes over nothing at Clacton and Margate, between 'Mods' and 'Rockers', pepped up by pills. Rising divorce rates, falling marriage rates, debunked moral hypocrisy. Loneliness in old age. Free love. No illegitimacy in children. Boredom in the young. The fear of loss of youth in the adult. The fear of death, which no labour-saving devices can remove. The fear of atomic destruction. Protestants or Catholics, nobody *really* believes in God. Nobody *really* cares about almost anything.

The instability of relationships and the fear of destruction have led to a seeking of refuge in sexual love. The overwhelming thought in the European cinema today is that love between the sexes is somehow more than sex, that even where it expresses itself solely through sex, there is a spiritual residue which redeems the individual, and saves him from death. In *Hiroshima mon amour* sexual love becomes the symbol of all love, and is pitted against the forces of destruction which are immortalized in Hiroshima. In Fellini's *La dolce vita* the monster from the deep in the dawn on the seashore after the dissolute night, is confronted by the innocence of the young girl, pitifully inadequate, yet a symbol of love which will save somebody somewhere.

But this is not the only reason for the preoccupation with sex in the European cinema of our time. How are human beings to express themselves ? How will they reveal their inner attitudes, their contradictions and fears ? Not through their relationship with God or to social ideals. In the act of love the human being is demasked; he is least protected from examination. In the very fundamental activity, something of himself is revealed. In Alexandre Astruc's *Crimson Curtain,* the young soldier in the ecstasy of love finds his girl suddenly dead in the midst of the very act. His love for this individual outside of himself turns, slowly and brutally, into fear for his own safety, love for himself alone. He drags the dead body around like a sack of potatoes, looking for a place to hide it. Finally he escapes. In Bergman's *Naked Night,* the personality of the leader of the circus is revealed most at the moment when his wife's infidelity is exposed to the world in the very shower of blows her lover rains on him. In the absence of God or of hunger, sex provides the most fundamental human activity in which attitudes can be held under a microscope.

Tourist mythology has built up France as the land of love. At least in the cinema, it is true. No other cinema has expressed so much of the sweet heartache of love, its lovely anguish, its fascinating despair. Truffaut's *Jules et Jim* does for the sixties in France what *Les Enfants du paradis* did for the period during the Occupation. The Jeanne Moreau of today was the Arletty of yesterday, and there is not all that difference between Jules and Jean-Louis Barrault. The mythology of love envelopes both. Both films have the headiness of champagne, keeping one resolutely on the lunatic fringe. In both, love saves one from the total annihilation of the soul. In Truffaut's film, World War I stands for the same thing as Hiroshima does in Resnais' *Marienbad;* is the same sort of *Pandora and the Flying Dutchman's* story of timeless love, expressed more deeply than the Anglo-Saxon ever could, his limit having been reached in *Brief Encounter.* Through endless corridors, of time as it were, the lover goes on pursuing the fleeting white shadow of the beloved in a dream-world where last year and this year and next year become one, and the real and the unreal become totally indistinguishable.

The shadowy search and the finding in the moonlight garden of *Les Amants* is the same intense longing to find deliverance of the soul in an everlasting embrace. The knowledge that the embrace cannot be everlasting, that a lifetime of love must be compressed into a few hours or days, that there is no *final* fulfilment in desire, and that ecstasy is in the longing itself, lends poignancy to these films. Jazz blues express this longing perfectly, albeit in an Italian film, in the restaurant sequence of *La notte.* But it is not confined to the mood of the blues. In Paul Eluard's poetry, the beloved becomes the symbol of the motherland; in Resnais it becomes concern for issues, not only in *Hiroshima,* but in the Algerian aspect of *Muriel.* Today's *Cahier du Cinema* describes the French quest as only a fascination with life; but I for one, do not believe that in the French preoccupation with love, there is no sense of concern for the individual. Even the prostitute in *Vivre sa vie,* made by that hero of *Cahier,* Jean-Luc Godard, is compared to the saint in a sudden excerpt from Dreyer's *The Passion of Joan of Arc.* There is compassion in the shots of the impersonal hands reaching for the body in the half-lit hotel room, of the towel on the rack, the soap-dish on the washstand, the coat neatly laid on the coat-hanger. The fascination with life theory reaches a new height in *Bande à part,* but even in this crime drama there is little of the Hitchcock whom Godard so perversely admires; a girl gets caught up with two amateur criminals; everything that happens is unexpected and yet one comes away with the feeling of having observed people caught up unthinkingly in the meshes of fate, primarily because they do not know where they are going, and do not care.

What, one might ask, is new in all this ? Neither the anguish of love, nor the sense of drifting existence is the discovery of the cinema. Indeed, there is nothing new in the basic themes as such. But in art the importance of style is in the fact that only style can be really new. The style is the artist; it is his manner of feeling which separates his emotions from the emotions of all others who have said the same thing, and makes it original. The truth of his statement is expressed in the intensity of the invention of technique. The New Wave is not all technical bravura; its need for invention arises from the unchanged character of its statement. Besides this, government control over scripts in the financing of films in the Centre National de la cinematographie tends to draw art away from the field of protest. I was told by many in France that it is impossible today to make a film even on the Dreyfus episode, not to speak of Algeria — Godard's film on which was banned. If there is an overemphasis on style in the French cinema it may have stemmed from this. Officials feel a certain amount of hesitation even in showing *Hiroshima mon amour,* because France is making atomic bombs herself. Yet there is no doubt that the innovations of the Nouvelle Vague have sprung from the need to intensify what statements it does make.

11

The transition from what I have called objective humanism to the exploration of the individual demanded a shift in the technical attitudes as well. The narrative derived from literature no longer satisfied the artist. It was not enough even to know what was happening in the mind of a character; what became more urgently felt was the need of greater freedom in achieving the subjectivity of the artist himself. In Ray's trilogy, we find a marvellous ability to bring out the events within the mind of the character (this is even more marked in some sequences of *Jalsaghar*), itself an advance on the ability to do so which Italian neorealism exhibited. The emotion which assails us as the orphan boy follows his adopted mother's hearse in *Miracle of Milan* is still wedded to the objective situation; it is far behind the evocation of *Jalsaghar* or Jeanne Moreau's wanderings through the streets of Milan in *La notte*. In *Jules et Jim* the inner feelings of the characters themselves are in fact of less importance than their creator's direct communication of feelings to the audience. The characters are used more as a means to that end than in the films of Ray or Chukhrai.

The objective reality of the existence of Jules or Jim is of far less consequences to Truffaut than of Apu to Ray or of the young soldier to Chukhrai. This is even more true of Resnais in *Hiroshima, Marienbad,* or *Muriel*. They seek as direct a communication in the cinema as the writer can achieve in literature. Hence their jump-cuts, in which there is no desire to follow the logical mental progresses of their characters; the audience is forced to follow the mind of the director and not of the creatures of his imagination. They move at his will, only to illustrate his meaning. Hence, too, the new literature. What is *Marienbad* or *Jules et Jim* without words ? French cinema has always been literary; it has few films like *Postmaster* or *Virgin Spring* or *Childhood of Ivan*. Going back further, one could not find in it the equivalent of the great laconic Westerns of the American cinema or the completeness in visuals of *Rashomon* or *Bicycle Thieves*. Today's 'literariness', however, is not at the expense of the visual; the words of *Lola* are by themselves trite, it is only the images which give them some fresh meaning. The text of *Marienbad,* beautiful as it is, would again be no more than a degenerate Pierre Louis, without the visuals. A new marriage of literature and the cinema is celebrated in the Nouvelle Vague, dashing all orthodox theories to the ground. No wonder Resnais has been called the James Joyce of the cinema. Cocteau's *Orphée* had been heavily literary in its symbolism, but never achieved the unity of word and image as in Resnais or Truffaut. This new addition of the power of words could cause headaches to critics of the cinema like Nicola Chiaromonte who judge the cinema's power of subjective expression solely by the juxtapositioning of visuals. The new French cinema goes to the extent of using visuals as illustrations at times, and yet reveals new cinematic truth in doing so. Eisenstein saw in the cinema 'a synthesis of the essence of all previous arts', and demonstrated this in *Ivan the Terrible.* Contemporary French cinema provides fresh proof of the truth of his statement.

I have spoken of the French cinema in discussing the attitudes and techniques in the West because it seems to crystallize them more powerfully than say in Britain or the United States. Critics have been baffled time and again in their attempt to find trends in the British cinema; Satyajit Ray probably hit the truth when he said that it is too wedded to craftsmanship to develop any trends. The only field in which Britain showed any was in the 'golden age of the British documentary' in the portrayal of 'man against the sky', its somewhat romantic observation of common man. Emotionalized by the tensions of the war, it produced its *Brief Encounter, Great Expectations, Odd Man Out, Henry V,* briefly lighting up the British virtues of understatement, fortitude, quiet pride in history and institutions, to fall back later, in the Ealing comedies, on its sense of humour and its ability to laugh at itself. Then came the 'angry' films in the wake of the plays, but again the promise died out, reasserting itself in a quieter form of anger in films like *A Kind of Loving* and *A Taste of Honey. But Tony* Richardson suddenly turned to *Tom Jones,* bringing out a lusty facet of the British tradition but belying the promise of a consistent development of a personal theme or of the cohesion of British film-making around a social one. Digs at the caste system of English life or essays on the greyness of working class affluence soon petered out to diverse attractions in craftsmanship in *Becket* and *Lawrence of Arabia* and *Tom Jones.* Ray quoted Reed as having said once that he was prepared to make a film on any subject as long as it made a good script. One fears that has once more become true of the British cinema, even with the younger generation of film-makers.

Of the new Italian cinema, we in India have only seen *La dolce vita* in a badly cut version as the example of the period since neorealism. Although I had the good fortune to see the whole of Fellini's film as well as his earlier *La strada,* Antonioni's *La notte* and Pasolini's *Mama Roma,* the ice is still too thin to skate. Both Fellini and Antonioni seem to ponder European moral values deeply, although one does so in baroque splendour as in *La dolce vita,* and the other in the gentle melancholy of *La notte.* *La strada* is an immensely powerful film in a fairly traditional idiom about an animal of a circus performer who in the end dimly perceives the moral consequences of his action. It seems obvious that Antonioni is the stylist in it who, along with the Nouvelle Vague, has most helped to expand the language of the cinema and to lead it into the deeper recesses of subjective expression. I could not see anything, in *La notte,* of the elements of 'anti-film' of which he has been accused by inane, and mostly literary, critics. Antonioni's films do not have the restlessness of the Nouvelle Vague; his contemplative style is too slow for the taste of many in Europe. It is far more akin to Ray's, although his subjectivity is greater. His camera dwells on the face for what might seem an eternity in which we become aware of the mutest notes of ambivalence of the character. In comparison, Fellini seems too flamboyant and showy in a sort of self-induced frenzy, often brilliant but equally often descending to symbols of Christ dangling from a helicopter. But in both, the era of neorealism is equally over, and the content of their cinema enters a new phase under the impact of affluence on Italian society.

Will American cinema ever find its Antonioni ? At least not in the junk heap of Hollywood studios decaying in disuse. Hollywood gave the lead towards spectacle in its effort to save the commercial cinema from the ravages of television. With the exception of a Hitchcock or a Wyler or a Kazan, even craftsmen have lost their freedom in Hollywood, and must turn out *Ben Hur* or *Fall of the Roman Empire* in order to survive. The home of the world's best average film can no longer afford its previous indulgences. No wonder serious film-making has fled to New York, and even Kazan has to repair to the East Coast. Yet the American conscience is far from dead, as the new trend of political and social problem films like *Judgment in Nuremburg, Advise and Consent, The Best Man, David and Lisa, One Potato, Two Potato* go to show. In the meantime, a new technique is taking its birth in the 'direct cinema' of the younger East Coast film-makers, presenting a new facet of the impact of television in its rough and ready style of shooting slices of life unglamorized by the polish of the big studios. Serious film-making in America needs no obituaries yet, but it still seems to be unsure of itself, its attitudes of social consciousness seem frothy and superficial in comparison to Europe. Even the vacuum in faith which it shares with Western Europe has not produced deep enough reactions in the minds of its film-makers.

Cinema in Eastern Europe seems to be in a state of transition, almost exactly reflecting the changes in its society. With its increasing affluence and its assertion of the individual against the restraints of Stalinism, it is emerging from the social straitjacket and turning more towards the individual as against the type, and towards personal expression rather than the embroidery of officially prescribed patterns. Most marked of all in Poland, the trend away from the glorification of the trench-hero is also making itself felt in films like Bulgaria's *Sun and Shadow,* the Hungarian *House on the Rock,* Czechoslovakia's *Crik,* which have more than the merely negative virtues of non-conformism, and have a freshness of content as well as of technique. Some of these films in fact misfire, unlike the ones named, by leaning over backwards in trying to prove to themselves that they are no less free than the French. In the USSR itself, a whole new series of films with a new humanist outlook have come out, *Letter That Was Not Sent, Childhood Of Ivan,* which do much more than show that free films can be made in the Soviet Union as with films like *Forty-First,* or even *Cranes Are Flying* with its ecstatic copy of out-dated camera tricks of the West. A mature aspect of Soviet cinema, as always is in its adaptations from literature like Yutkevitch's *Othello,* Herifetz's *Little Dog* and Kozintzsev's *Don Quixote.* But compared with the Polish cinema, the USSR's self-expression is still naive, and despite the note of neohuman-ism in some of its films, the Soviet individual, in the cinema at any rate, is only halfway out of its chrysalis. The 'thaw', we hope, has only just begun.

It would be fascinating to trace the patterns of transition in Japan from feudalism to modernity by studying its cinema. The blend of East and West in today's Japan would be an equally rewarding study. And Japanese cinema with a produc-tion of some four hundred films distributed in six thousand theatres must surely reflect something of the mind of the country ? Despite the reported strength of commercial con-siderations in a cinema which has increased its audience in an age of television, there has been no lack of artists. Kuro-sawa is of course the best known because of *Rashomon,* that brilliantly Shakespearean and contemporary essay on ambiva-lent human behaviour in late mediaeval Japan. A not dissi-milar theme is developed in Teshigahara's *Woman of the Dunes* which earned much praise in Cannes. The film shows a school teacher with a passion for studying insects, who falls captive to a mysterious lonely woman engaged in a daily strug-gle with nature, and chooses to go back to this captivity imme-diately after he has escaped from it. It reminds me of the ghost woman of Mizoguchi's *Ugetsu Monogatari,* although the poetry here is of a different kind. In all the three films — and they sum up my recent experience of Japanese cinema together with *Street of Shame* and *Sansho Dayu,* both by Mizoguchi — the mystery, the eternal attraction, the capacity to bear suffering, to be the pivot of existence, emerge as the hallmark of woman. Mizoguchi in particular seems to create a world in which woman is the still centre, whether she is mother or beloved or both, round whom man restlessly re-volves, trying to prove his prowess. There is something very close to basic Indian attitudes in this, although Mizoguchi's

films have none of the naiveté of overt statement which afflicts
the average Indian film-maker specially when he is dealing
with the role of woman.

But that is perhaps where any similarities between Japanese
and Indian cinema ends. For in India, everything recedes in
the face of the monumental problems of poverty and ignorance,
and there is not only scope but need for a humanism which
does not appear so obviously in Japan in her oriental affluence.
The strength of Satyajit Ray lies in the very fact that he is able
to detach himself from the immediacy of these problems and
is able to view the fundamental change in the life of the country
as a whole over a long period of time. The total absence of
the agitational approach in Ray makes him an Antonioni of
humanism (terrible as the phrase is) in his mood of contemplation in the midst of chaos, as it were. There is a sense of
identification of the modern Indian with the condition of the
masses from whom he is so far removed in every respect in
the rigidly classified society of India. His heroes are the young
Tagores, steeped in Indian tradition but reaching out to the
modern world and Western thought. The Apu trilogy and
the decaying landlord of *Jalsaghar* or the superstitious Kali-
worshipper of *Debi* are all equally of India in transition, viewed
with sympathy and resignation, and a quiet faith in the inevitability of change, a total absence of cynicism.

What affluent India will be like nobody knows; perhaps
we shall have the same problems of loneliness and vacuum
in faith: but at least for the present, the goal of realising
material happiness for the country gives modern Indian
thought a new spirituality and a sense of faith. In the work
of the better directors, therefore, there is a complete involvement in the human condition, and a 'Stand Up! Stand Up'
call is totally unnecessary. In fact the urgency of social problems creates some dissatisfaction with the lyrical propensities
of Ray in those who would rather see him grapple with his
themes in a more dramatic and directly involved manner. Even
the meanest of Indian film-makers makes the recurring gesture
to social causes, and there is naturally some impatience with
the seemingly remote attitude of one of the world's finest film
directors towards the problems of his country. Whether such

impatience will result in the emergence of new, powerful voices in the cinema or not we have yet to see. In the meantime it is obvious that for any such emergence, a hermetical sealing off of Indian cinema from all outside influences can only act as a preventive. To attract new talent and to generate fresh forces, the windows of Indian cinema must be opened out wide on the world. That is the task of international film festivals of India and, on a day to day basis, of film societies.

1965

notes on
Russian cinema

The grand passion of faith which the Russian cinema has celebrated since the revolution has not been without a touch of self-immolation. As in all such communal dedication to a faith, the cinema developed something of the character of religious art. Communism, like Christianity, has been presented in many facets by scores of artists, from the most brilliant to the pedestrian, over a few generations, on the walls of the new churches of a technological age — the cinema theatre. From Vertov to Tarkovsky, a span of half a century has seen artists with varied temperaments disciplining within a given framework the expression of their emotional, intellectual, artistic and technical predilections. That is why the Russian cinema, even at its worst, has never become frivolous; it has never abandoned the objectives of its social environment to become either commercial in its conformism like the American cinema or nihilist in its nonconformity like the French.

But the canons of religious art, practised in an age of science and self-consciousness, have suffered somewhat from the tortuous involutions of a forced surrender of the self to the ideals of the state — both where the force has been an external inquisition and where it has come from the fear of the sin of inner nonconformity. Eisenstein the intellectual, Dovzhenko the poet, and Pudovkin who shared something of the qualities of both — all suffered from the need to restrain, divert, realign their natural artistic impulses. Perhaps for this reason, Russian cinema has attained something of the strength, but little of the innocence, of faith in all but a few of its very large output of films. The myth-like quality of the American

Western or musical has never touched the Russian cinema; made vociferously for the people, it has remained, in the main, a cinema of the intellectual elite. Its mass public today, an eighty million a week, is reported to delight in the American product and the offerings of the Hindi cinema rather more than in the work of the native cinéaste.

The beginnings of its sombre involutions may perhaps be traced as much outside the revolution as within it. The earliest influence to which it was subjected was the Nordic; Denmark and Sweden had cinemas bearing national characteristics before the twenties. The earliest Russian films had titles which speak for themselves — *The Nail on the Coffin, The Four Devils, The Tragic Wager, The Club Of the Blasé with Life.* The subjects of these films, made in the early years of the century, were drawn mostly from the Nordic and were as sombre as that indicates. A look at Stiller's *Sir Arne's Treasure* (1919) shows the sources of the composition style of Eisenstein, thought to have been solely his own, until early Scandinavian cinema was re-examined in the film museums of Europe.

One line of the deep Nordic trait went to Germany and found fertile ground there in the postwar despondency, to create the 'Expressionist' school with its stylised exaggeration, its taste for the macabre which fulfilled its tortured soul. The other had already reached into Russian cinema and was to be transmuted and partially absorbed into its revolutionary ardour. To see the early films of Fritz Lang today is to realise that they are not without some correspondence in their composition and their penchant for the drama of violence, with the early revolutionary cinema of Russia. Despite the difference in purpose, the dramatic power of *Potemkin* derives a lot from the spiking of the woman's eye, the shooting down of the woman and child, the rolling down of the perambulator, the limping flight of the beggar. In the slitting of the bull's throat in *Strike,* the lifting of the bridge with the dead horse in *October,* there is an unmistakable flair for the violently dramatic. And whenever either Eisenstein or Fritz Lang protographed a bridge, one could trust both to shoot it from below, going in a diagonal across the screen.

Without pushing the correspondence too far, it may be observed that *Potemkin* shows little concern for the child hurtling down the steps to its very individual death; after all, it was the mass which was the hero. In Vakulinchuk's death, the tears shed are, if such an expression may be admitted into our parlance, 'ideatic tears'. When Kuleshov experimented with a shot of Mosjukin, juxtaposing it with close-ups, first of a plate of soup, then of a coffin, and finally of a child, the unsuspecting audience discovered in Mosjukin's unaltered expression the *ideas* of hunger, of mourning, and of affection. What in a continuous shot would have been an observation of life became, in montage, an abstract idea. Kuleshov gave the cinema an additional dimension and the Soviet film an instrument for abstracting itself from the particularity of the event. In Eisenstein's hands, Kuleshov's invention became a powerful means of creating 'ideatic emotion'. He himself proceeded to the musical dimension, aided by the variation of the length of a piece of film in relation to the length of the one to which it is juxtaposed. There are passages in *Potemkin* which are truly full of an unheard music, so rhythmical are the movements within a shot and from one shot to another. *Potemkin* is a perfect, powerful and moving work. But one has a faint suspicion that if Eisenstein had applied his analytical-creative brain power to the fantasies of a deranged mind like Caligari's, he would have been more successful than Wiene. It is interesting to note that as early as 1923, he had in fact done the montage for the Russian version of *Dr Mabuse*.

Eisenstein's theoretical writings bring out the nature of his concerns. He was in many ways a laboratory scientist, a super-craftsman whose main passion was to subject the film medium to constant test more in order to discover the essence of the medium than to express his own attitudes and feelings towards reality. Of all the great film-makers of the world he was probably the most concerned with the *art*. The brilliant chapters on 'Synchronisation of the Senses', 'Colour and Meaning', 'Form and Content in the Film Sense', show the extraordinary extent to which his creativity was *conscious*. The logic of every shot, every movement, is explained in clear-cut diagrams and mathematical formulae, in which the interpolations of socialist dogma sound a jarring note. Many have seen in the figure of *Ivan the Terrible* a portrayal of Stalin who was a symbol of the mental torture which Eisenstein suffered over the abandonment, at State behest, of *Bezhin Meadow,* the criticisms against him of formalism and exaggerated research, indirectly fused with his bitter disappointment over the debacle of *Que Viva Mexico.* He poured all of himself into this great film which achieves what he had always aimed at : the cinema as the culmination of all the arts. The second part of the film travels far away from socialist dogmas and any attempt to reconcile them with the artist's inner urges. In fact except perhaps in *Potemkin* he probably never brought art and the revolution perfectly together. But he had cared then; later he did not.

In varying degrees, what was true of Eisenstein was also true of the others. Georges Sadoul finds Kuleshov's application of the results of his Mosjukin experiments in *According to the Law* (1926) 'close enough to Expressionism' in the excessive, contortionist ecstasy of the actors. The most enduring outcome of Dziga Vertov's insistence on actuality has been in the Cinema Verité in France. In the Soviet Union itself, the trend he set got lost in the emphasis on stylization.

Pudovkin's was a less complicated personality; his search for the individual in relation to the mass — the mother in *Mother,* the hesitations of the English soldier ordered to kill the Mongol in *Storm over Asia* — resulted in a somewhat more directly emotional concern. But the theoretical-technical preoccupation was by no means absent, as evidenced by the much-discussed cutting between the stock exchange and the fighting at the front in the *End of St Petersburgh.* This self-conscious preoccupation with art led to *Deserter* (1933) which 'was criticised by a group of Leningrad workers who found it too intellectual for their taste. The criticism disturbed Pudovkin, and it had a valid basis. The intellectual quality of his work does not lie in the psychological emphasis which rarely goes beneath the surface, but in its arrangement of incidents to convey abstract or symbolical meanings — like the martial music imposed on the demonstration in the Hamburg streets' (John Howard Lawson, *Film : The Creative Process*). This failure of his theory of contrapuntal sound so disheartened him that for several years Pudovkin retired from direction into teaching. When he was in India (was it in 1949 ?) he read a long, cloudy treatise on socialist realism, waxed enthusiastic over a Calcutta Film Society showing of *Storm over Asia,* and grimly announced that he was going to make a film to prove that the Russians had been the first to invent the aeroplane. With him was the magnificent actor Nikolai Cherkassov (*Nevsky, Ivan the Terrible, Don Quixote*) who embarrassed his over-political admirers by declining to recite Mayakovsky and sticking to Pushkin instead. His recent death brought to a close the brilliant career of an actor with a god-like presence and a golden voice.

Even Dovzhenko, the peasant poet of the Russian revolution who came nearest to its 'innocence', was not free of the conscious preoccupation with artistry and with dramatic violence. Nor was he a poet of the masses. His silent films remain almost impossible to understand without subtitles, so keen is their search for allegory, symbolism and metaphor. At the end of *Arsenal* (1929), the dead heroes of the revolution continue to march; the murder and the funeral are the supreme moments of *Earth* (1930); his *Ivan,* which I have not seen, Sadoul found extremely obscure.

But if the great Russian directors did not achieve a simple unity with the people, and if their work remained uncomfortable in that knowledge, divided between their devotion to art and their wish to serve the revolution, what they did achieve was not only a number of masterpieces (*Potemkin, Ivan the Terrible* Pts I & II, *Mother, Storm over Asia, Earth*) but an enormous expansion of the language of the cinema. It is as cinéastes rather than as revolutionaries that they remain memorable.

The sound period began with a bang. Nicolai Ekk's *The Road to Life* (1931), a film of great sincerity was also one of the few to have made such brilliant use of sound so soon after its debut. But by now Stalinism had the cinema firmly in its grip. The number of productions dwindled from 104 in 1928 to 40 in 1939; the lowest wartime figure was 21 in 1943, but by 1951 it had dropped to a mere 8. Quality suffered no less than quantity. The only films which reached a really high level in the thirties were the three films on Gorki by Mark Donskoi (1938-40), perhaps the greatest film biography ever made. The forties were equally bleak, except for Eisenstein's two-part film on *Ivan the Terrible* (1944-46), the second of which ran into so much trouble with the state that it was not released until 1958. Chiaurelli's pseudo-epic *Fall of Berlin* and Petrov's *Battle of Stalingrad* (both released in 1949) had moments of grandeur in what was basically devoted to the cult of the Stalin personality. Neither Pudovkin (*Suvorov*, 1941; *Nakhimov*, 1946) nor Dovzhenko (*Michurin*, 1948) scaled any great heights in their biographies.

It was not until the 'thaw' that both the number and the quality of films began to pick up again. Film production rose steadily, reaching its peak with 140 films in 1958, a figure which has been maintained in recent years. In 1956, Chukhrai made history with *Forty-First*, by making a touching film on a woman soldier who falls in love with her prisoner, an 'enemy of the people'. In the same year, Kalatozov caused an equal sensation with his *Cranes Are Flying*, a sensitive, highly non-political study of a woman in love. Yutkevitch had already made a successful Shakespeare adaptation in *Othello* (1955); 1959 saw Chukhrai's *Ballad of a Soldier*, a film of great simplicity and charm if not profound depth; by 1960, Heifetz had made one of the finest achievements of the Soviet cinema in his nostalgic, exquisite adaptation of Chekhov's *Lady with the Little Dog*. Tarkovsky's film of the lost childhood of a boy-spy during the war, *Childhood of Ivan* (1962), gave further evidence of the new, deeply human concern for the individual in the Soviet cinema; and in 1964, Kozintsev made what is probably the finest Shakespeare film yet seen, *Hamlet*, using Pasternak's prose translation. Bondarchuk completed his mammoth *War and Peace* in 1965, 'perhaps the most ambitious, beautiful and exact transposition of literature to the screen yet undertaken'. These films have been a direct outcome of the loosening of the state's stranglehold on art which came with the early years of the Krushchev regime; they are yet hesitant feelers out into a new world of unfettered creativity. The *freedom* of expression does not yet go to the extent of the Polish and more lately, Czech films like Milos Forman's *Loves of a Blonde* in which a film is no longer a product of ideology but of essential humanity and the creative impulse. Perhaps that is why the finest achievements of new Russian cinema are still in the sphere of adaptation of classics. But there is no doubt that unless the process of liberalization of thought is reversed, Russian cinema is once more poised for great development.

1966

In a Personal Vein

ﾞﾞ from advertising
to films

I have often wondered why so many advertising people end
up in films — although not all of them are as successful in
it as Satyajit Ray.

Like Ray, Rajen Tarafder (of *Ganga* fame) was an art
director in an advertising agency before choosing to be a film
director instead. In a long line of succession to them came
Arup Guha Thakurta (*Benarasi*), O. C. Ganguly (*Kinu Goalar
Gali*), Purnendu Pattrea (*Swapna Niye, Stir Patra*); Shyam
Benegal, who had made some fine documentaries before leaving
advertising. I wandered into it, too : I made a film on the
city of Calcutta for the Calcutta Film Society before leaving
advertising — *Portrait of a City* — highly praised by a critic
who, misled by an acknowledgement to Satyajit Ray, had
thought it was by him.

In an odd way of its own, advertising demands an absorption of literature, the arts and the contemporary world as does
the cinema. Eisenstein described the cinema as 'the culmination of all previous arts'. Whether this definition is over-
ambitious or not, the fact is that the cinema derives a lot from
painting, literature, music, dance, and even architecture, and
photosynthesizes them under the hard light of science and
technology.

Yet there must be something very frustrating about advertising to lead so many of its practitioners out into filmdom. Perhaps it is the end result. Advertising must remain as exhorta-
tion to buy tea or tyres, cigarettes or bicycles, soap or switchgear.
A director may find films, sometimes, to be an embodiment of
personal expression which communicates itself to others, per-

haps even endures.   In the jargon of personnel experts, it can
bring 'more job satisfaction to the incumbent'.

There is no doubt that it does, almost regardless of results.
Auguste Renoir once said that there is no fun in sleeping with
a prostitute; the fun is in looking for her.   The comparison
does not go all the way, though, because nothing delights a
film-maker more than when his film is enjoyed by others and
what he felt is felt by a large number of people.   That is show
business.   And there is no business like it because the events
leading up to public acclaim are so absorbing and exciting
that even when the acclaim does not come, people go on
enjoying the process of looking for it, and hoping that this
time it will work.   Of course, failure brings depression, but
it is like the hangover of the morning after, which never prevented anybody from going on a binge again.   Even the let-
down is a part of the excitement; in show business it is the
intensity of feeling that matters — whether it is of the jubila-
tion over success, the death-wish after failure, or the boredom of long periods of waiting.

One of the undoubted rewards of documentary film-
making — one that studio-bound features do not offer, nor
even bits of location work in affluent style — is the one of
getting to know one's country.   Today you may be working in
an art museum, tomorrow in a village in Haryana; you may
spend a week or more in a Himalayan hamlet, eating the local
food and sleeping where you can, or you are for days in a
desert in Rajasthan, in a fishing village in the south.   Where-
ever you go, you see people, of different kinds, speaking different tongues, at close quarters.   Besides what you put into
your film, you discover a lot about people and their ways,
much of it you had not suspected, in spite of all that you may
have read.   Sometimes this knowledge can have more depth
than that acquired by a journalist investigating a story because
film-making, with all its waiting for the right light and the
complex coordination of people and things, is a more time-
consuming process.   Even in the cities, places that you thought
you know can throw up surprises when you look closely at
them for the purpose of making a film.

Shooting at various museums for *Dance of Shiva,* a film

on Ananda Coomaraswamy, quite often the lighting of a piece of bas-relief would literally bring to light unsuspected features in the work. So much so that sometimes museum officials would themselves wonder at the transformation of the relief. Expressions would leap up in the eyes and lips of the tiny faces; faint inscrutable smiles across the ages that faded away as soon as the bright, rightly angled light was switched off.

It took me several miles and almost a whole day of scouring the Kangra valley to find the long spiked flowers that one sees so often in Kangra miniatures for the same film. On a previous visit I had seen similar flowers and was convinced that exquisitely artificial as they looked in the paintings, they were not products of the artist's fancy but imitation of nature around. Apparently, the season was not right. But we did find not a plant but a tree with long bare branches with spiked flowers. They were not quite what I had wanted but similar enough to make a good prelude to the Rajput paintings sequence built around Coomaraswamy's wanderings in that area.

However, filming people is perhaps more satisfying than art or flowers. The sheer creative vitality of a person like Birju Maharaj, for instance, makes the process of getting to know him as fascinating as that of making the film. His responses are so quick and his movements so deft that it is a pleasure to watch him dancing, teaching, singing, playing the tabla, the mridangam, or any of the variety of things at which he is so adept. At a moment's notice he breaks into dance, or song, switches to playing an instrument — not only in his familiar surroundings but in a broken temple, an unknown palace or anywhere you land him. Sitting at a moviola, he helped me edit the dance shots, and was quick to understand the requirements of the film medium and accept, for the sake of it, any necessary incompleteness in the representation of the dance. In making a film on a dancer, it is necessary to strike a certain balance between the interest of the film as a film and as a representation and record of the dance. Birju Maharaj composed brief but rounded pieces of music and dance which brought out many aspects of his art and allowed the time, within twenty minutes, to establish something of his personality, his art inheritance and his family life.

He was delighted with the cinematic gimmick of the last sequence of the film, in which constant cuts are made between him dancing in Moghul and in Hindu costumes and styles, in a sort of 'sawal-jawab' (question-answer) style. For lack of a comparable shot, I had included a small bit of dancing at the end of which he gestures to ask me if what he was doing was all right. It was in rhythm, but, strictly speaking, not a part of the dance ! He realised at once that I needed that shot, there being no alternative to counterpoint the piece before it. I had feared that it would take long explanations to make him agree to accept it. But I did not have to waste words; he was quick-witted, as usual, and agreed, taking a childlike pleasure in the process of cutting from one piece to the other.

Too often in India, documentaries on art are confused with the art of the documentary. Watching me take a lot of pains over an industrial film, a senior Films Division man once said to me : 'Why are you wasting so much time on this ? Make a film on a sentimental subject, and you will win a prize.' When I asked what he meant by 'sentimental', he explained that it should be on a temple or some such 'sentimental' subject. One of my favourites among my own films is an early one I made on the crossing of a river by ferry boat, early in the morning, by people, trucks and cars which have been waiting for various hours from the previous night. It is a slow, painful, and sometimes dangerous crossing at the end of which the camera quickly swings up into the sky following a crane, and shows a new bridge across the river, nearing completion. Many film-makers praised the film; it was shown at the Museum of Modern Art, New York, and at the Robert Flaherty Seminar and had good reviews. But it found no buyer in India, and one member of a committee, a well-known dancer, whose powers of film appreciation are not as developed and intuitive as Birju Maharaj's, said that there was nothing 'artistic' about it.

There is another kind of judge, or buyer, of films who demands a clearly delivered and preferably wordy 'message'. The intellectuals are usually of this kind; they can respond only to ideas and not to things. Their excitement, emotions are all derived from an interplay of abstract ideas, of statistical or journalistic facts treated as things. They are concerned with the ideatic mirror image of reality, not reality itself. Typically, they get agitated over the idea of the indiscriminate felling of trees leading to soil erosion, but cannot get fascinated by a particular tree and try to understand it, in the way a painter would 'understand' it. These are the intellectuals without sensibility whose name is legion. They get impatient when the camera dwells on a face or explores a landscape; they are satisfied only when they can find an instant 'meaning' in blandly literary terms. Even those among them who have literary or musical culture, find it impossible to relate it to their experience of film which gets blocked rather than enriched in the process.

Their influence on the Indian documentary has been nothing short of disastrous, because unlike the feature, the documentary in our country is not made directly for the public but for the people who decide what the public should see. The intellectuals among them, insensible as they may be, are nothing compared to the diehard bureaucrats who have somehow slipped into positions requiring a quality of judgement they will, alas, never have. Its absence, however, will not prevent them from building their empires with reinforced concrete, pouring it into every little gap in the structure that insulates them from the real world, and from ideas or feelings.

Probably the kind of documentary that teaches the film-maker most is the one that explores some aspect of poor people's lives near him, or far away, but equally unfamiliar to him in his educated, and superior, city-bred ways.

A film I once shot in Delhi concerned a tailor, a cobbler, and a crowd of shopkeepers, chauffeurs and ayahs gathered around them every morning, in Nizamuddin West, under a tree. The tailor reads a newspaper, and the others listen. Sometimes he adds his own explanations; sometimes he answers a question. He sits on the pavement under the tree; behind him is a park, and next to him the cobbler sits and repairs shoes. One by one the shops open, chauffeurs go off to take their sahibs to the office, ayahs to feed the children. The tailor goes to open his shop, and sits down at his machine.

Only the cobbler remains at his spot, under the tree. The group breaks up — but not before the newspaper has been heard from the very first line to the last.

Apart from the interest of the scene, so meaningful in to-day's India, I was struck by the quiet dignity of the tailor. He was not only the local intellectual, but his manner and bearing were so self-possessed, so full of poise without vanity, that one could not help admiring him. Many people have wondered at the dignity of the common man in India in all his suffering; but it had never come home to me so much as when making a film with him. What a wonderful medium the cinema is for conveying this dignity; I remember seeing *Report on Drought,* a moving documentary (by Kapil and Vaidya) on the early days of the Bihar drought, before relief organisations from all over the world had descended on it. The quiet expression of endurance on their faces — unexcited, unsentimental — made the impact unbearable. Even when asked a question on their condition, they replied with eyes averted, voices dispassionate. 'Calm without; fire within', as Satyajit Ray said in an essay on the cinema in the East.

One sees, while making documentary films, not only the dignity in the face of suffering, but the suffering itself. Even without calamities, the daily grind is telling enough. In a village only twenty miles from Calcutta, within three miles of the railway track and two miles of a bus route, we waded through knee-deep slush for half-a-mile along a village road to reach the point where it was breached some years ago. Men, women and children get down from the train and walk one and a half miles of a slippery mud track, breached a little here and there, wade through the knee-deep slush for half-a-mile only to reach the piece de résistance, the place where for about fifty yards they must walk through chest-deep water to get up on the other side to resume the journey.

After a while there is another breach, and then the footpath finally leads one home — every day, morning and evening. For something like ten square miles, the vast field enclosed by the railway embankment on the side and the semicircular road on the other, the accumulated rain water has no outlet. The villages are like islands, except for the slushy footpath.

One of the villages we went to has no drinking water, the tube-well having given up its ghost a few years ago. Children go out in little boats scooped out of coconut trees to fetch water from the next island-village. The paddy stands in chest-deep water, the grain harvested is hardly four maunds per bigha, and the plants produce no hay, rotting in the water which does not dry up until about March.

It is because the documentary-maker sees these sights all the time that he is so often in conflict with authority. He aches to bring the injustice, poverty and oppression he observes to light; he wants to record the truth as it is. But the establishment is forever afraid of the truth; it wants to project the so-called positive image. It is not bothered about the fact that such undiluted 'positive' projections, an euphemism for falsehood, are simplistic and therefore incredible. Besides, by telling the audience regularly every week that everything in the country is fine and the few remaining problems are just about to be solved, they are putting the conscience of the city-bred, who make up the large majority of the cinema audience, to sleep. Yet it is the privileged classes in the cities who wield the power to do something about the problems of the common man. If a medium as effective as the documentary film is not allowed to rouse his conscience, then what purpose does it serve except to paint a rosy picture and help keep the party in power ? Most audiences find the pictures so patently incredible that they walk out for their colas and cigarettes as soon as the familiar insignia appears on the screen.

The documentary-maker who wants to shake up the audience by presenting the naked, unpalatable truth runs into instant trouble. The only way he can survive is by conforming to the mores of propaganda that passes for 'documentary'. The ones that cannot, die — like K. S. Chari. Chari and Abraham's *Face to Face* had once caused a sensation by presenting the actual views of the man in the street on India's democracy. Even though the outcome was 'positive' and the film credible, films of this kind, which flowed briefly during the tenure of Jehangir Bhownagary as Chief Adviser on cinema to the Union Government of India, were pushed out of existence by irate politicians and bureaucrats.

So if you ever have the urge to feel close to Indian realities, just walk to your nearest Nabagram, and make a documentary of it.   It won't do your conscience any harm.

1972

dance of Shiva: postscript to a film

In the course of an interview for the film, Dr. Sherman E. Lee, director of the Cleveland Museum of Art, said : 'If Coomaraswamy had been alive today, he would have become a culture hero for the younger generation.' Indeed, I made my rediscovery of Coomaraswamy not through his writings on art, but through some of his essays on the state of the modern industrial civilization. Years ago, I had read his *History of Indian and Indonesian Art* and *The Dance of Shiva*. I had known vaguely that he had been associated with the cultural reawakening in this region, but over the years my image of him had narrowed down to that of a scholar whose work had become somewhat mildewed milestones in the study of Indian art.

It was when I came across a paperback reprint of his *Christian and Oriental Philosophy of Art* that, turning its pages, some fragments caught my eye : 'One of the most obvious characteristics of our culture is a class division of artists from workmen.... We have come to think of art and work as incompatible...and have for the first time in history created an industry without art.' He went on to speak, in this address at Harvard University in 1937, of today's 'exaggerated standards of living and depreciated standards of life.... It is one of the greatest counts against our civilization that the *pleasures* (italics mine) afforded by art, whether in the making or of subsequent appreciation, are not enjoyed or even supposed to be enjoyed by the workmen at work.... It is taken for granted that while at work we are doing what we like least, and while at play what we should wish to be doing all the time.... The craftsman likes talking of his handicraft, but the factory worker likes talking of the ball game.... An industry without art provides a necessary apparatus of existence — an apparatus lacking the essential characteristics of things made by art, the characteristics, viz., of beauty and significance.'

I began to read more of Coomaraswamy and discovered that this Harvard address 'Is Art a Superstition or a Way of Life ?' elaborated on a theme that had begun in his early writings in Ceylon around 1904. I also found that I had not been alone in my ignorance of the larger social significance of his work and in regarding him merely as a great art scholar and pundit. More than a generation had lost touch with his social philosophy and its relevance to our times. When he frequented India in the 1910s and 1920s he had been regarded as a vital part of the cultural resurgence of that era, and not just as an art scholar. But in later years, he became increasingly to most people a scholar of Indian art living in the United States. His work became more and more confined to the world of scholarship, more particularly scholarship in Indian art. And that cloistered world, while acknowledging him as a master in the interpretation of art, paid scant attention to his idea of society which arose from his idea of art. It is only recently that his work has begun reaching a wider public through paperbacks; as a social philosopher, he is coming into his own. A rediscovery of Coomaraswamy has become imminent.

I was therefore not surprised at Dr. Lee's comment about Coomaraswamy and the younger generation. I had rediscovered him from that angle anyway, and had already resolved someday to make a film on the man. The true significance of his work had been forgotten, and had to be held up to the world and especially to India once again. Perhaps a film could contribute something to this task.

No wonder then that the question my co-producer director B. D. Garga and I had to answer most frequently wherever we went was : Who is this Ananda K. Coomaraswamy ? Through frequent repetition, our answer reached a telegraphic leanness of form : 'He was a Ceylonese of Indian origin born of an English mother, brought up in England and trained in geology. But he wrote more than 500 publications on Indian and Asian art, most of them in his 30 years at the Boston Museum, and became its greatest single interpreter and also a social philosopher of significance.'

I was in Boston in 1968, and went to see Donna Luisa Coomaraswamy, Ananda's fourth, and last, wife. She was then working on a definitive edition of his works sponsored by the Bollingen Foundation. A common friend, Robert Steele, professor of film at Boston University, took me to see her. When I announced my plans for making a film on her husband, she fell silent. I waited anxiously to know if she was going to cooperate. All Coomaraswamy's photographs, manuscripts, records and other memorabilia were with her, and without her help it would be virtually impossible to make the film. She had herself taken numerous photographs of him, having been a well-known photographer. In fact, it was as a photographer that she had first made Coomaraswamy's acquaintance.

After a while she looked up and asked me : 'Have you had any education, young man ?'

There have been numerous occasions in my life when I have been at a loss for words. This was certainly one of them. But Donna Luisa was not going to give up. She looked on, and waited. Suddenly intelligence dawned on me. I managed to remember and recite a verse in Sanskrit from the Mahabharata. My rusty Sanskrit saved the day.

She said : 'All right, I will help you. What do you want ?' I said money, because I had not yet found a sponsor. She did not have any, nor did she have any ideas on where I could find some. But we became friends. It was a sad moment for me when a year later Robert Steele wrote to say that she had died.

Talking about sponsors reminds me of my poor effort to convince someone in authority of the worthiness of my project. This person was knowledgeable on art, so I had high hopes of him. But after hearing me out he said something that shattered me and once again left me speechless : 'How can you make a film on him ? He was so dull.' My intelligence did not make even a late start; too dumbfounded to

reply, I lost a potential sponsor. Years later, the reply oc-
curred to me. No man who had four wives and numerous
admirers among beautiful women could be called dull.

He was more than six feet tall, handsome and distinguished.
Mrs. Margaret Marcus, herself an art expert who lives in Cleveland, remembered him vividly. 'He had the lanky grace of a
cowboy,' she said. 'He loved fishing and was a very good
cook. Also a good photographer. He once cooked me a
curry that was so hot the top of my head hit the ceiling.'

'All his wives had to do something,' Mrs. Marcus continued,
'Ethel translated Ceylonese classics. Alice, whom he renamed
Ratan Devi, sang Indian classical music — to the satisfaction
of Rabindranath Tagore. Stella danced Indonesian dances.
Zlada, who called herself Donna Luisa or something, was a
professional photographer.'

Mrs. Marcus showed us exquisite drawings of Stella made
by Coomaraswamy and also some photographs taken by him.
The drawings were nudes, twenty-eight of which were published, and had nothing to do with Indian tradition. They
were nearer, rather, to sketches made by Rodin or Maillol before sculpting a figure. All of them in the book were not
equally successful. But the ones collected by Mrs. Marcus,
with her own unerring judgement, were exquisite. The photographs my cameraman Purnendu Bose enthusiastically approved of were wintry landscapes. Mountains dimly discernible in the mist seemed to exercise a fascination for him.

To the suggestion that Coomaraswamy was a dull man,
Mrs. Marcus shook her wiry old head violently, and for a
long time.

Ananda's son (by Donna Luisa) Rama, a heart surgeon at
a hospital in Greenwich, Connecticut, revealed to me Coomaraswamy the film-maker. I cursed myself as I carried the
heavy 16-mm projector across the overbridge at the Greenwich
railway station. It was so heavy that I could hardly walk.
Rama was busy throughout the day and yet so anxious to help
that he had given me an appointment for the night. After
dinner at the beautifully sited local club, his wife Bernadette
took leave of us, and Rama and I settled down to an all-night
session of talking, identifying and dating innumerable photo-

graphs and seeing Ananda K. Coomaraswamy's films. The first one was on a bullfight in Spain, shot sometime in the late twenties. I sat up. There was nothing amateurish about the tones, or about the way the camera was moved. Everything had been shot from one point of view — the spectator's fixed seat — but the excitement of the event had been captured so well that one did not feel the sameness. Another was on the geishas of Japan. This one had detailed subtitles describing the function of the geisha and explaining the meaning of her actions. There was another which Coomaraswamy had shot in South India, in which aged devadasis demonstrated mudras from Bharata Natyam. And then there were many of Ananda himself vacationing in Maine, where he went every year. Some of these showed a fine feeling of landscape. I particularly remember a long-lasting beautiful shot of a horse swimming.

Rama and his wife are ardent Catholics, but he did not see any real difference between his father's beliefs and his own. We agreed on many things, disagreed on others. Finally I went to bed. 'At ten, Francis will wake you, and Bernadette will drive you to the station at quarter to eleven when she takes the children to school.' Francis, who looks like an angel, shyly woke me in time. As Bernadette waited in the car, while hauling the projector downstairs I fell and sprained my ankle. I limped to the car and decided not to say anything about it. At Grand Central Station in New York, I took the risk of leaving the projector on the platform and went to find a porter. When we came back, the projector was still there. I limped throughout the rest of my stay in the United States. But the discovery of the films had been beyond my wildest dreams. No, Ananda Coomaraswamy was not a dull man.

One of Coomaraswamy's oldest and most consistent admirers is Dorai Raja Singham, a schoolteacher who lived in Ceylon for a long time but later set up home in Kuala Lumpur in Malaysia. In fact 'KL' was my first port of call and the object was solely to meet him. Some years ago Dorai Raja Singham had published two volumes of homage to his guru, containing tributes from scholars all over the world. All through his life he has collected each scrap of paper he could

get on Coomaraswamy, corresponded with him and practically
everyone who had known him. At present he is preparing
a volume of Coomaraswamy's letters. We pored over his
collection in his peaceful home at Kuala Lumpur, photographed
letters and sketches, and listened to his account of the man
whose commemoration has become the mission of Dorai
Raja's life.

It was he who first introduced me to the manuscript of Roger
Lipsey's voluminous book on Coomaraswamy published by
Princeton University. It is not only a biography but a detailed assessment of his work, written after a great deal of
research. Lipsey had sent his manuscript over to Dorai Raja
Singham for him to check the facts and in turn checked the
facts I was to narrate in the film. I read his manuscript
before finalizing the narration. But more than that I was
glad to find at last an authoritative biography written of a
man who hated biographies as far as he himself was concerned
and always refused to give details of his personal life, extol-
ling invariably the anonymity of the Indian traditional artist
as his ideal.

I suppose making a film about a man is a little like writing
his biography. Although the film is more of a documentary
on his work than on his life, in finding out about him, in trying
to understand him, I had to take the attitude of a biographer.
You begin to understand your man only when you begin to
see the contradictions he tried all his life to resolve or perhaps
to ignore. Many writers and great men emerge to us all of a
piece, adding up to a consistent 'image'. When you know
all or most of his aspects, including the hidden ones, you begin
to feel a special relationship with him. Your knowledge of
his weaknesses not only does not diminish, but actually enhan-
ces the warmth of your feeling for him.

One of the contradictions of Coomaraswamy's life arose, I
feel, from the distance between him and the home of the art
he loved. In his salad days he was an ardent social reformer,
a man committed to the cause of his country's regeneration.
'I thought how different it might be if we Ceylonese were...
not ashamed of our own nationalities,' he had said. India was
his spiritual home. Writing in his *Essays on National Idealism*

he had said : 'I do not believe in any regeneration of the Indian people which cannot find expression in art; any reawakening worth the name must so express itself.' He was studying the traditions of a culture with whose present reality he was deeply concerned and closely connected. Over the years, however, India and Ceylon became more than memories; they became idealized in his mind and unrelated to the struggles, the agonies, and the compulsions of these countries. He did not live to see the growth of independent India. He would have disapproved of much of what we are doing today. He would probably have said, as he had said in 1910, that it will matter much whether the great ideals of Indian culture have been carried forward or allowed to die. It is with these that Indian nationalism is essentially concerned, and upon these that India's fate as a nation depends. He would no doubt have hated the advent of the plastic bucket. Yet he would have been a part of the struggle, trying to make his voice heard with a sense of urgency and immediacy which distance eventually removed. He lived in America's present and in India's past. That is why towards his later life, his statements on the future of uncontrolled industrial materialism rang true, being close to the living reality. His spirit remained universal whether he spoke of the dangers of the proliferation of human wants instead of the refinement of their quality or of the dangers of imitative materialism overwhelming India's special message to the world. But his understanding of present-day India became too dim for his statements to retain much relevance. Similarly his glorification of India's past became increasingly uncritical and unrelated to historical fact. Not only India's present but India's past grew more and more mythical — more of a state of mind than a statement of history.

In this transition there must have been a secret agony which some of the photographs of him in the late thirties betray.

Another contradiction lay in his opposition to industrialism and his enthusiasm for medieval craft society. Coming years after William Morris, the scientist in him must have known the impossibility of actually reviving the medieval structure of society. As early as 1904 he had sought a way of life for our land which would remember the old wisdom and yet not

13

despise the new. Even in urging India to remain true to her heritage, he had never specifically asked her to shun industry. But he never faced up to the basic contradiction in his medievalist posture, and if he did attempt to resolve it, he never spoke of it in his work. He showed no way to a new synthesis between science and tradition. In his early years in Ceylon and in India there is some suggestion of his acceptance of the Tagorean ideals of synthesis; but in his later years, probably because he was so far removed from the realities of these newly independent countries, his accent is solely on medievalism on the one hand and condemnation of industrial society on the other. Where he did say something valid for the younger generation in America was in his criticism of the state of society rather than in prescriptions for a way out of its impasse. In this he is no different from other critics of a society in danger of being swept off its feet by an accelerating rate of change in science and technology.

The value of his social philosophy lies more in the acuteness of his analysis of what industrial society does to the individual — an analysis made in the early thirties. In regard to the future, he had no particular vision of what was likely to come about, but held up the values which higher social organization must provide.

Reading his poems, looking at his drawings of nudes, his photographs, his motion picture photography of bullfighting in Spain or of himself fishing in the Maine woods, the photographs of his wives — German, English, American and Argentinian — one can conjure up an image of Coomaraswamy opposed to the well-known image of him as a bearded Oriental savant. It is as if these images were two sides of a coin with East printed on one and West on the other. It was always the Eastern side that was more visible to the world. The metaphor should not be pushed too far, because his writings show indeed a fusion of an Oriental intuition with the scientific discipline of the West; but behind the surface unity of his life and work it is impossible not to detect a core of unresolved contradictions.

If Coomaraswamy did not project these contradictions in his writings, it was not merely in order to present a unified image.

It was due more to his dislike of the glorification of the individual. He never wanted to analyze the artist as a special kind of man; his ideal was man, anonymous, yet always 'a special kind of artist'.

I am no expert on art, but I had to try to understand what made Coomaraswamy unique among art scholars. It was, I think, the totality of his vision. He was able, unlike many scholars, to relate art to language, literature, history, philosophy and religion. Not only to so relate it consciously, but simply to see it as an integral part of human endeavour at the given time and in the given society. He did not believe in art for art's sake; his theory of art was utilitarian. An image of God is an aid to contemplation just as a water pot is an aid to the job of carrying water. To all who believed in this, it was impossible to separate the beauty of art from the inner harmony of the society that produced it. It was thus essential to explore the relationship of art to the other functions of society. In this lay his advantage over many Western scholars of Indian and Eastern art who, basically unable to penetrate the other disciplines, have to confine themselves largely to a discussion of art in isolation from the totality of the culture.

Where he scored over Indian scholars was in his knowledge of the West and in his scientific training. The reports he wrote as the director of mineralogy in Ceylon have the same precision in the marshalling of facts and the logic of conclusion that his work on art shows. An example of this is his classic *History of Indian and Indonesian Art.* In less than 300 pages he wrote the most effective survey of all phases and aspects of Indian and Southeast Asian art ever brought into a single work. The wide range of his knowledge across East and West enabled him, in his own words, to 'use one tradition in order to illuminate another'. He began as a nationalist seeking to re-establish the glory of the Indian tradition. His means were as scientific as his expressions were controlled; yet in proving to the conference of 400 Orientalists assembled in Copenhagen in 1908 that the Buddha image had originated in India and had not been imported from Hellenistic sources, there must have been a quiet sense of national pride. But when he spoke at the celebration of India's Independence in Boston in August 1947, he said : 'Indian culture is of value to us not so much because it is Indian as because it is culture.' He had risen above all national chauvinism. The student of art must cease to be a provincial; he must universalize himself. Human individuality is not an end in itself, but only the means.

A good part of Coomaraswamy's work was obsessed with the differentiation of Indian art from art in the West, and much of what he said seems self-evident today. In his early years, the individuality of Indian art could be brought out only by that differentiation. Scholars of Indian art were at that time invariably European and mostly British; they saw it peopled by many-armed and hydra-headed monsters with the little that was good in it such as the Buddha image, derived from second-rate Hellenistic models. Coomaraswamy had to strive to show not only the worth of Indian art but its individual identity as an expression of a distinct civilization. To the marked change that came about in the world's knowledge and understanding of Indian culture over the years, no single man had contributed more than Ananda K. Coomaraswamy. Yet, having made this monumental achievement, he saw all culture as 'dialects of the same language'. This is unlike so many later scholars who built on foundations laid by him but never got rid of their regional chauvinism.

But the rediscovery of Coomaraswamy is no longer as important to India in the area of art as it is in the understanding of art as an index of social organization. It is as a social philosopher that his work can provide a cultural leadership to an India that is in danger of losing the important values of Indian tradition and may be hurtling, by a combination of choice and necessity, towards the ills that beset industrialized societies. Ananda Coomaraswamy should thus become a culture hero for the younger generation in India as much as in America or anywhere else.

1973

෨ a select bibliography

Balasz, Bela, *Theory of the Film,* New York: Dover, 1972.

Barnouw, Erik and Krishnaswamy, S., *Indian Film,* New York: Columbia University Press, 1963.

Bazin, Andre, *Jean Renoir,* New York: Simon and Schuster, 1973.
——*What Is Cinema?* Berkeley and London: University of California Press, 1971.

Eisenstein, Sergei M., *Film Form and Film Sense,* New York: Harcourt, Brace, Jovanovich, 1969.

Eisler, Hans, *Composing for Films,* New York: Books for Libraries, 1971.

Hardy, Forsyth, *Grierson on Documentary,* New York: Praeger, 1971.

Jacobs, Lewis, *The Rise of the American Film,* New York: Harcourt, Brace, Jovanovich, 1968.

Kracauer, Siegfried, *Theory of Film: The Redemption of Physical Reality,* New York: Oxford University Press, 1965.

Pudovkin, U.I., *Film Technique and Film Acting,* New York: Grove Press, 1970.

Richie, Donald, *The Films of Akira Kurosawa,* Berkeley and London: University of California Press, 1980.

Sarkar, Kobita, *Indian Cinema Today,* New Delhi: Sterling, 1975.

Seton, Marie, *Sergei M. Eisenstein: A Biography,* London: Bodley Head, 1952.

Sontag, Susan, *Against Interpretation,* New York: Delta, 1967.

Warshow, Robert, *The Immediate Experience,* New York: Atheneum, 1970.

ɷ a select bibliography

Balasz, Bela, *Theory of the Film,* New York: Dover, 1972.

Barnouw, Erik and Krishnaswamy, S., *Indian Film,* New York: Columbia University Press, 1963.

Bazin, Andre, *Jean Renoir,* New York: Simon and Schuster, 1973.

—— *What Is Cinema?* Berkeley and London: University of California Press, 1971.

Eisenstein, Sergei M., *Film Form and Film Sense,* New York: Harcourt, Brace, Jovanovich, 1969.

Eisler, Hans, *Composing for Films,* New York: Books for Libraries, 1971.

Hardy, Forsyth, *Grierson on Documentary,* New York: Praeger, 1971.

Jacobs, Lewis, *The Rise of the American Film,* New York: Harcourt, Brace, Jovanovich, 1968.

Kracauer, Siegfried, *Theory of Film: The Redemption of Physical Reality,* New York: Oxford University Press, 1965.

Pudovkin, U.I., *Film Technique and Film Acting,* New York: Grove Press, 1970.

Richie, Donald, *The Films of Akira Kurosawa,* Berkeley and London: University of California Press, 1980.

Sarkar, Kobita, *Indian Cinema Today,* New Delhi: Sterling, 1975.

Seton, Marie, *Sergei M. Eisenstein: A Biography,* London: Bodley Head, 1952.

Sontag, Susan, *Against Interpretation,* New York: Delta, 1967.

Warshow, Robert, *The Immediate Experience,* New York: Atheneum, 1970.

✌ index

A Propos de Nice—93-94
Aarohi—91
Abasheshe—85
Abhijan—59, 73, 81
According to Law — 172
Achanak — 34
Achut Kanya — 11
Adhe Adhuray—88
Advise and Consent—10, 44, 165
Agragami Group — 90
Ajantrik — 36, 80-81, 83, 149
Akash Kusum—13, 85, 87, 89
Akutagawa, Ryunosuke—119
Alexander Nevsky — 143, 173
All-India Conference of Film Societies —100
All India Radio—34-35, 104
All Quiet on the Western Front—152
Amants, Les—160
Amateur Cine Society—96
American in Paris, An—146
American Tragedy, An—129
Amiche, L'—132
Anandam—99,101
Anderson, Lindsay—21, 95
Anita—8
Anstey, Edgar—94
Antariksha—90
Antonioni, Michelangelo—38, 69, 107, 112, 130-132, 156, 158, 164, 167
Anupama—10
Aparajito—57-58, 71
Apu trilogy—56-57, 59, 68, 72, 131, 167
Apu Sansar—57-58
Aristarco, Guido—130-131
Arsenal—158, 173
Arundhati Devi—14
Ashes and Diamonds—158
Asphalt Jungle—105
Astaire, Fred—146
Astruc, Alexander—159

Atithi—91
Azmi, Kaifi—31

Badauni, Shakil—31
Baiju Bawra—146
Baishe Sraban—84
Balachandran, S.—31
Balika Bodhu—14
Ballad of a Soldier—158, 174
Ballet Mechanique—94
Bande à Part—161
Bandyopadhay, Bibhuti Bhushan—57, 132
Bandyopadhyay, Manik—73
Banerjee, Kali—60, 81, 84, 88
Banerjee, Nikhil—79
Banerjee, Tarashankar—73
Baptista, Clement—97
Barnouw,Eric—52, 93
Barrault, Jean-Louis—150, 160
Barua, Pramathesh—15, 49, 51, 54, 70
Battleship Potemkin—94, 96-97, 116, 118, 125, 131, 142, 170-173
Bazin, A—87
Becket—164
Belle et la bete, La—24, 154
Ben Hur—165
Benegal, Shyam—179
Bergman, Ingmar—44, 69, 112, 129, 158-159
Berlin : Symphony of a Great City—93
Best Man, The—10, 44, 165
Bezhin Meadow—157, 172
Bhagat, Usha—99
Bhaskaran, P—15
Bhatia, Vanraj—36-37
Bhattacharya, Abhi—82
Bhattacharya, Ajoy—32
Bhattacharya, Basu—10
Bhattacharya, Bijon—88
Bhonsle, Asha—33
Bhuban Shome—37, 86, 88-89

Bicycle Thieves—125, 137, 162
Big Country, The—145
Big Store, The—148
Bilet-Pherat—78
Bindur Chheley—50
Birju Maharaj—118, 181-182
Birth of a Nation—156
Biswas, Chhabi—60
Bombay Talkies—11
Bombay Film Society—96
Borinage—94
Bose, Debaki—54, 90
Bose, Modhu—54
Bose, Subhas Chandra—74
Breathless—96
Bresson—107
Bridge, The—93
Bridge on the River Kwai—153
Bridges of Toko-Ri, The—153
Brief Encounter—115, 151-152, 160, 163
British Federation of Film Societies—95
British Film Institute—95
Brussels Cine Club—94
Bunuel—156
Burman, Ashish—85
Burman, Sachin Dev—31-32

C.I.D.—152
Cahier du Cinema—160-161
Cahier du Capitaine Georges, Les—129
Calcutta Film Society—85, 97-99, 142, 173, 179
Cardiff, Jack—137
Carné, Marcel—20, 150
Cartier-Bresson—114
Cavalcanti—135
Centre National de la cinematographie—161
Chakravorty, Tulsi—148-149
Chalachal—91
Chalachitra—98
Champion, The—147
Chandidas—90
Chandralekha—14
Chaplin, Charles—19, 54, 104-105, 112, 118, 120, 125, 127, 129, 140, 147, 156-157
Charitrahin—50
Charulata—13, 37-38, 58-59, 63-65, 69, 71, 73, 80, 119, 131
Chatterjee, Anil—61, 66, 82
Chatterjee, Saratchandra—50-51
Chatterjee, Soumitra—57-61, 63, 73, 81, 88
Cherkassov, Nikolai—97, 143, 173
Chhayasurya—92
Chhinnamool—97-98

Chiaromonte, Nicola—163
Chhuti—14
Childhood of Ivan—158, 162, 166, 174
Children's Film Society—101
Chitralekha Film Society—99
Chowdhury, Partha Pratim—92
Chowdhury, Salil—31-32
Chowdhury, Shanti—36
Chowdhury, Supriya—82
Chukhrai, Grigori—158, 162, 174
Cine Central—99
Cinema—95
Citizen Kane—112, 119
Club of the Blase with Life, The—170
Coastal Command—135
Cocteau, Jean—24, 129, 154, 157, 163
Coomaraswamy, Ananda K.—181, 187-192, 194-196
Coomaraswamy, Donna Luisa (Zlada)—189-190
Coomaraswamy, Rama—190-191
Cooper, Gary—144
Cranes Are Flying—166, 174
Crik—165
Crimson Curtain—159
Crown Unit—135
Cry of the City—152

D. G. (Dhiren Ganguly)—78
Daddy Long Legs—146
Dak Harkara—90
Dance of Shiva—180
Das, Jibanananda—72, 77
Das Gupta, Hari Sadhan—13, 92, 97
Datta, Sudhindranath—77
David and Lisa—165..
De, Bishnu—77
DeMille, Cecil B—119
De Sica, Vittorio—125, 137, 158
Debajan—57, 132
Debdas—49, 51-54, 78
Debi—58-59, 61, 63, 67-68, 80, 83, 167
Deep Jele Jai—91
Delluc, Louis—95
Deserter—172
Dickens, Charles—126, 159
Dieterle, Wilhelm—143
Do Bigha Zamin—10, 78
Dolce vita, La—43, 159, 164
Don Quixote—166, 173
Donen, Stanley—10, 146
Donskoi, Mark—174
Dovzhenko, Alexander—158, 169, 173, 174
Dr. Mabuse—171
Dreiser, Theodore—129
Dreyer, Karl—15, 54, 112, 116, 118, 161

𝒶 index

Drifters—93, 134
Drishti Film Society—100
Dupont—118
Dutt, Guru—54, 78
Dutt, Utpal—79, 86

Earth—173
Eisenstein, S—15, 24, 54, 94, 112, 116-118, 120, 125, 127, 129-131, 143, 157, 163, 169-172, 174, 179
Eki Ange Eto Roop—92
Ekk, Nicolai—173
Eliot, T.S.—77
Elstree—53
Eluard, Paul—160
End of St. Petersburgh—172
Enfants du paradis, Les—150-151, 160
Evening in Paris—7

Face to Face—42, 185
Fall of the Roman Empire—165
Federation of Film Societies of India (FFSI)—99-101
Fellini—43, 69, 101, 112, 158-159, 164
Film—95
Film and Photo League—93, 95
Film and Television Institute—100-101
Film Comment—95
Film Enquiry Committee—106
Film Rutan—95
Film Society, London—93-96
Film Society of Lincoln Center—95
Film : The Creative Process—172
Filmliga—93, 96
Films Division—35, 42, 94, 99, 139, 182
Flaherty, Robert 20, 94, 134-135, 137
Fonda, Henry—144
Ford, John—9, 15, 20, 104, 108, 112-113, 120, 144, 156
Forman, Milos—44, 175
Fort Appache—144
Forty-First—166, 174
Four Devils, The—170
French Cine Club—93
French Federation of Film Societies—95
Friendly Persuasion—19, 145

Gandhi, Indira—99
Gandhi, M. K.—4, 23, 41, 46, 55, 58, 72-73
Ganga—13, 90, 92, 179
Ganga Jumna—8
Ganju, J. N.—98
Ghatak, Ritwik—13-14, 36, 38, 80-84, 87-88, 92, 97, 99, 149
Ghosh, Nimai—97

Ghosh, Pannalal—79
Giant—145
Go West—148
Godard, Jean-Luc—3, 96, 103, 107, 131, 133, 161
Gold Rush, The—19, 118, 125, 140, 142
Goopi Gain Bagha Bain—12, 88
Gora—56
Gorki, Maxim—174
Grande Illusion, La—158
Great Expectations—126, 163
Grierson, John—93-94, 134, 139
Griffith—104, 157
Guha Thakurta, Arup—13, 179
Gujral, I. K.—99
Gupta, Hemen—99
Gupta, R. P.—98

Hamlet—19, 68, 122, 174
Hands—93
Headmaster—90
Heifetz—166, 174
Heiress, The—145
Henry, V—163
Heston, C—145
Hercules—156
High Noon—144
Hill, Samuel Berkeley—97
Hiroshima mon amour—117, 156, 158-162
Hitchcock, Alfred—10, 53, 104-105, 152, 161, 165
Hollywood—9-10, 20, 79, 91, 95, 103-105, 113, 120, 127, 140, 152, 164-165
Hollywood Stuntmen Association—108
House on the Rock—165
Housing Problems—94
Houston, Penelope—95
Huston, John—105

Images d' Ostende—93
India 1967—42
Indian Film—52
Indian Film Culture—16, 100
Indian Film Quarterly—100
Indian Film Review—100
Indian People's Theatre Association (IPTA)—32, 80-81, 83-84, 88
Indrapuri Studio—98
International Film Festival, 1952—92, 98, 150
Intolerance—19
Ivan (Dovzhenko)—173
Ivan the Terrible—116, 119, 143, 157, 163, 173-174
Ivens, Joris—93

Jagirdar—54, 143
Jalsaghar—59-61, 63, 66-68, 71, 73, 83, 146, 149, 150, 162, 167
James, Henry—145
Jancsós—101
Jayakanthan, D—15-16
Jeffries, Derek—96
Jhanak Jhanak Payal Baje—10
Jivan Prabhat—11
Juarez—143
Judgement at Nuremberg—10, 44, 165
Jules et Jim—85, 160, 162

Kabuliwala—91, 155
Kaghaz Ka Phool—54
Kalidas—41, 83
Kalpana—34-35, 98, 146
Kamasutra—41
Kanal—158
Kanchanjangha—60
Kanoon—34
Kapoor, Raj—10
Kapurush—59, 64-65, 73
Kar, Ajoy—91
Kariat, Ramu—15
Karma—78
Kaufman, Boris—94
Kaye, Danny—148
Kazan, Elia—165
Kelly, Gene—146
Khan, Ali Akbar—36, 79, 83
Khan, Ustad Nissar Husain (Senior) —118
Khan, Vilayet—36, 79
Kind of Loving, A—163
Komal Gandhar—81, 83
Konaraka—97
Kozintzsev—166
Kracauer, Siegfried—114
Kripalani, Krishna—99
Krishnaswamy, S—15-16, 52
Kshaniker Atithi—90-91
Kshudita Pashan—36, 91
Kuleshov, Lev—171-172
Kumar, Dilip—78
Kumei, Fumio—93
Kurosawa, A—25, 69, 112, 153, 156, 166

Lady with the Little Dog—166, 174
Laksmikant-Pyarelal—32
Lambert, Gavin—95
Lang, Fritz—152, 170
Last Year at Marienbad—117, 160, 162-163
Laurence of Arabia—164
Lean, David—115, 126, 151, 153
Lebedeff, Gerashim—79

Léger, Fernand—94
Lejeune, C. A.—135-136
Leprohn, Pierre—132
Letter That Was Not Sent—165
Leyden, Rudy von—96
Life from out of the Ruins—136
Light of Asia—78
Lola—162
Lorentz, Pare—94
Louis, Pierre—163
Lubitsch, Ernst—104
Lumière Brothers—119

Mahabharata—23, 189
Mahanagar—43, 61-62, 64-65, 73-74, 85
Majumdar, Kamal—98
Majumdar, Tarun—13-14
Makavajev—107
Mama Roma—164
Man of Aran—134
Mangeshkar, Lata—32-33
Marx Brothers—147-148
Marx, Chico—148
Marx, Groucho—148
Marx, Harpo—148
Marx, Karl—158
Matira Manisha—13-14, 85-89
Mature, Victor—152
Meghe Dhaka Tara—38, 81-83
Mejdidi—50
Méliès, Georges—119
Mifune, Toshiro—153-154
Milestone—9, 152
Ministry of Fear—152
Minnelli, Vincent—10
Miracle of Milan—162
Mitra, Shambhu—79
Mitra, Subrata—97
Mizoguchi, Kenji—158, 166
Moana of the South Seas—94, 134, 141
Modi, Sohrab—143
Moitra, Jyotirindra—83
Monsieur Verdoux—147
Montage—99
Mother—96, 158, 172-173
Moreau, Jeanne—160, 162
Moussinac, Leon—95-96
Mukherjee, Gnyanesh—88
Mukherjee, Hemanta—31-32
Mukherjee, Hrishikesh—10
Mukherjee, Madhabi—63, 73
Mukherjee, Sandhya—32
Mukti—51, 53, 78
Mulay, Suhasini—86
Mulay, Vijaya—99
Mullick, Pankaj—32
Muni, Paul—143

Muriel—160, 162
Museum of Modern Art, New York—182

Nagarik—80
Naked City—152
Naked Night—159
Nanook of the North—20, 134, 141
National Film Archive of India—100
Neelakuvil—15
Nehru, J. L.—4-5, 12, 41, 45-47, 55, 72, 106
New Theatres—32, 99
Nice Cine Club—93-94
Night at the Opera—148
Night Mail—138
Nil Akasher Nichay—84, 88
Nirjan Saikate—91
Notte, La—38, 130, 156, 158, 160, 162, 164

October—170
Odd Man Out—151, 163
On the Town—146
One Potato, Two Potato—165
Orphèe—163
Oshima—107
Osten, Franz—78
Ostende Cine Club—94
Othello—122
Othello (Yutkevitch)—166, 174
Oxford Film Society—95
Ozu—107, 119

Pabst—54
Paisa—137
Pajama Game, The—146
Palki—8
Pallisamaj—50
Panchatapa—91
Panchthupi—92, 97
Pandit Mashai—50
Pandora and the Flying Dutchman—160
Panigrahi—86
Parash Pathar—36, 60, 73, 148
Paramount—134
Paris nous appartient—157
Pasolini—164
Passion of Joan of Arc, The—54, 116, 118, 161
Pather Panchali—21, 35, 37-38, 43, 55-56, 66, 69-71, 80, 84, 87, 89-90, 97-98, 123, 125-126, 131, 149
Pati, P. Dr.—96
Pattrea, Purnendu—73, 92, 179
Pavese, Cesare—132
Pawar, Lalita—143

Peck, Gregory—145
Phalke, D.G.—78
Plow That Broke the Plains, The—94
Portrait of a City—99, 179
Postmaster—61, 66, 162
Prabhat Films—99
Pratinidhi—85
Proletarian Film League (Prokino)—93
Proust, Marcel—77
Pudovkin, V.I.—96-98, 158, 169, 172-173, 179
Punascha—36, 85
Pyaasa—54
Pygmalion—148

Que Viva Mexico—129, 157, 172

Raat-Bhor—84, 88
Rai, Himangshu—78
Rainbow—153
Ramer Sumati—50-51
Ramshastri—54, 143
Ramayana—76
Rao, Vijay Raghav—37
Rashomon—119, 125, 153-154, 156, 162, 166
Ray, Satyajit—4, 14, 36-38, 43, 57, 59-75, 80-85, 87-90, 92, 97-100, 107, 112, 120, 125, 131, 146, 148-149, 150, 162-164, 167, 179, 184
Rear Window—105
Reed, Carol—151, 164
Regle du jeu, La (*Rules of the Game*)—119
Reluctant Debutante, The—148
Renoir Auguste—67, 180
Renoir, Claude—97
Renoir, Jean—15, 18-19, 34-35, 68, 87, 97-98, 112, 119, 129, 144, 154, 157-158
Resnais, Alain—117, 158, 160, 162-163
Richardson, Tony—163
Riley, Ronald—137
River, The—34-35, 97
River, The (documentary)—94
Road to Life, The—173
Romeo and Juliet—146
Rossellini, R—137
Rotha, Paul—135
Ruttmann, Walter—93, 135

Sadoul, Georges—172-173
Sagar Sangame—90
Sagina Mahato—91
Saha, Barin—13
Saigal, K. L.—32
Samapti—58-59, 62, 67

Sangam—8, 10
Sansho Dayu—166
Sant Tukaram—54
Search, The—145
Searchers, The—144
Secret Life of Walter Mitty, The—148
Selznick—113
Sen, Aparna—88
Sen, Asit—91-92
Sen, Hiralal—78
Sen, Mrinal—13-14, 36-37, 84-88, 92, 99
Sen, Sobha—88
Sen, Subhas—98
Sequence—95, 97
Seton, Marie—98
Seventh Seal—126, 158
Shakuntala—10
Shane—145
Shankar, Ravi—35-38, 79
Shankar, Uday—34, 98, 146
Shantaram, V—10, 15
Sher-Gil, Amrita—55
Shirali, Vishnudas—35
Shoeshine—137
Shore—158
Shuna Baranari—91
Shyamchi Aie—155
Sight and Sound—21, 95
Signet Press—98
Silence—158
Silent Barricade—153
Sikander—143
Singham, Dorai Raja—191-192
Singing in the Rain—146
Sinha, Tapan—13, 36, 90-91, 122
Siodmak, Robert—152
Sir Arne's Treasure—170
Sitting Pretty—148
Sjoman—157
Sound Barrier, The—153
Spellbound—53
Srikanta series—50
Stage Coach—144
Steel—137
Steele, Robert—189
Steiner, Ralph—93
Sternberg, Josef Von—104
Stevens, George—145
Stiller, Maurity—170
Storck, Henri—93-94
Storm over Asia—97, 98, 172-173
Strada, La—74, 164
Strangers on a Train—152
Strike—131, 170
Street of Shame—166
Stroheim, Erich von—104, 120
Subarnarekha—81-83

Sucksdorff, Arne—99
Sultanpuri, Majrooh—31
Sun and Shadow—165
Swapna Niye—13, 92, 179
Swedish Federation—95

Tagore, Rabindranath—4-5, 8, 12, 37, 41, 45-47, 51, 55-59, 61, 64, 66, 69, 72-74, 77, 80, 82-83, 88, 91, 119, 190
Tagore, Sharmila—7
Tailler, Armand—96
Tarafder Rajen—13, 89-90, 179
Tarkovsky—107, 158, 169, 174
Taste of Honey, A—163
Teen Kanya—71
Teesri Kasam—10
Tero Nadir Parey—13
Teshigahara, Hiroshi—166
Third Man, The—151
Time—72
Timir Baran—35
To Light a Candle—36
Top Hat—105, 146
Tolstoy, L—123
Tom Jones—163-164
2001 Space Odyssey—103
Tragic Wager, The—170
Truffaut—66, 85, 103, 107, 112, 158, 160, 163

Ugetsu Monogatari—166
Ulanova, G—146-147
University of California, Los Angeles—97
Unnaipol Oruvan—15-16
Uski Kahani—10
Upanishads—42, 83

Vaijayanthimala—8
Van Dyke, Willard—93
Variety—118
Vasan, S. S.—14
Vavra, Otakar—153
Verma, Mahadevi—84
Vertov, Dziga—94, 169, 172
Vidor, King—113
Vigo, Jean—93-94
Vijaykar—97
Virgin Spring—44, 162
Viridiana—156
Vishva-Bharati—77
Vivre sa vie—161
Voyage to the Moon—119

Wagonmaster—144
Wajda—64
War and Peace—123, 174

Weavers of Maindargi—97
Watt, Harry—135, 138
Webb, Clifton—148
Welles, Orson—112, 119
Wiene, Robert—171
Wellman, William—105, 145
Woman of Paris—157
Woman of the Dunes—166

Wright, Basil—135, 138
Wyler, William—145, 165

Yellow Sky—105, 145
Yutkevitch—166, 174

Zils, Paul—96
Zinnemann, Fred—144-145